HOW TO
TAKE
TESTS

HOW TO TAKE TESTS

JASON MILLMAN

Professor, Educational Research Methodology
Cornell University

WALTER PAUK

Director, Reading-Study Center
Cornell University

McGRAW-HILL BOOK COMPANY

New York   St. Louis   San Francisco   London
Sydney   Toronto   Mexico   Panama

HOW TO TAKE TESTS

Library of Congress Catalog Card Number
69-16341

1213 FGRFGR 7983210

ISBN 07-048915-7

CONTENTS BY CHAPTERS

CONTENTS BY PRINCIPLES

7

SENTENCE COMPLETION ITEMS

8

OBJECTIVE TEST ITEMS

9

VERBAL ANALOGIES

INTRODUCTION

Many people earn lower scores on tests than their knowledge or aptitude warrants because they lack a sophisticated approach to taking tests, that is, test-wiseness. Test-wiseness is the ability to use characteristics of tests and test-taking situations to reach the full potential of one's knowledge and aptitudes. It is the importance we attach to having each individual's score accurately reflect his achievement and aptitude that is the reason for this book.

This book does not emphasize techniques of how to study, but rather concentrates on the principles of taking tests –both teacher-made and standardized. Our preoccupation with principles of *taking* tests does not mean that we believe studying is unimportant. Actually, the best way to prepare for an examination is to master the subject matter through thorough study and periodic review. Only then can a student walk into a testing room with confidence, for he will *know that he knows*. The student who seeks a quick and easy way to score high on examinations without serious study will find little help here. However, the student who wants his test marks to reflect his diligence and preparation should find this book especially rewarding.

There is a wide variety of tests ranging from subtle personality tests to matter-of-fact interest inventories. This book will focus mainly on two types of instruments: Those which test knowledge and those which test abilities. The items in both these tests have right and wrong answers.

The two main categories are *achievement* tests and *aptitude* tests. The first category, achievement tests, which include both teacher-made and standardized tests, is designed to measure how much a student has learned. The second category, aptitude tests, which are almost exclusively standardized tests, is designed to assess a student's potential. The difference between achievement and aptitude tests is that of purpose, but the items may frequently be similar.

Many principles of taking achievement and aptitude tests are presented and analyzed in this book. They have been gathered from various sources: interviews with hundreds of successful students, analysis of research on test construction, advice given in a number of booklets on taking tests, observation of students in test-taking situations, and experience gained from carefully controlled experiments.

Some of the principles of test-taking apply to all examinations and are frequently used by students who score high on tests. These include: using time wisely; reading directions and questions carefully; seriously attempting all questions, even those which *look* long and difficult; and checking answers for errors. Other principles apply more narrowly to the answering of special types of test questions or to the taking of achievement or aptitude tests measuring selected abilities.

Separate sections of this book emphasize how to answer special types of test items (for example, essay questions); other sections concentrate on principles of taking tests of selected abilities (for example, vocabulary tests). For further guidance, two tables of contents have been provided: The table of contents by chapters presents major topics and the table of contents by principles presents not only a detailed overview of the entire book, but also a quick source in concentrated form for finding particular principles and perceiving relationships among these principles.

To get the most out of this book, we suggest the following,

1. Read the principles carefully, making sure you fully understand them.
2. Study the illustrative examples.

3. Work out the examples and practice problems.

4. Refer to the appendices, when relevant.

Merely reading about the principles is not sufficient; you have to employ them by practicing the test-taking techniques until they come to you naturally.

Armed with the principles in this book, you will be able to do as well on tests as you should. In addition, you will finally be competing on an equal basis with those high-scoring students, no brighter or better-informed than you, whose only past advantage was their test-wiseness.

PART 1

PRINCIPLES
OF EXAMINATION
READINESS

The sophisticated test taker knows that being prepared for a test is the first step toward good test-taking techniques. In Chapter 1, Intellectual Preparation, principles designed to increase your competence in subject matter and aptitude are discussed; in Chapter 2, Emotional and Physical Preparation, suggestions are made for improving your attitudes toward the testing situation, for being mentally alert, and for controlling the tendency to tense up.

1.

INTELLECTUAL PREPARATION

Although the principles and techniques of how to take tests will help you along the road to success, you will fall far short of your goal unless you master the subject matter or acquire the needed aptitudes. To become mentally prepared, we recommend the following principles.

1.1 LEARN THE PROCEDURES FOR EFFECTIVE STUDY[1]

Much has been written about how to make the best use of study time, how to take good class notes, how to read with understanding, and so on. Since this book concentrates almost entirely on how to do well on tests, we suggest that you also read one of the many books on how to study.[2]

For immediate use, we present two study techniques: the first deals with how to master the textbook, and the second is concerned with how to master the classroom lecture. These two techniques have been chosen because most students would agree that to succeed in college you must be

[1] All the numbered principles presented in this book have been collected and placed in a separate table of contents found on pages vii to xii.

[2] See, for example, Walter Pauk, *How to Study in College* (paperback), Houghton Mifflin Company, Boston, 1962.

able not only to understand and assimilate the information from these two sources, but also to convert this information into knowledge.

To master the textbook, we suggest the OK4R Method of Reading, which is presented in a sequence of six steps. To master the classroom lecture, we suggest a technique which includes both a special note-taking format and a five-step procedure. (See both methods at the end of this chapter.)

1.2 STUDY WITH REGULARITY

Some cramming is undoubtedly beneficial, especially for reviewing and consolidating the more specific ideas and facts learned regularly during previous weeks. But to delay the initial learning of subject matter until just before an examination is foolhardy. The best advice is: Begin on the first day of classes to study and master each day's lectures and each day's assignments—not almost every time, but *every* day.

1.3 STUDY YOUR PAST QUIZZES AND TESTS

Analyze your strengths and weaknesses. If the weaknesses in a previous test were due to skimpy answers, for example, perhaps you did not take sufficient notes in class or read your textbooks in sufficient depth. In any case, find your past mistakes and correct them.

1.4 STUDY EXAMINATIONS GIVEN IN PREVIOUS YEARS

Familiarize yourself with earlier examinations. Learn not only what the correct answers are, but why they are correct by understanding the underlying reasons and principles. If you do, you will have the flexibility to apply such knowledge to forthcoming examinations. Remember that the identical questions may not be repeated, but the underlying concepts may be. After all, in any course or area of aptitude there are only a limited number of concepts and abilities to test.

Also familiarize yourself with the *kinds* of questions asked. Such familiarity can be a valuable guide as you study because it helps you to focus on ideas, facts, and abilities most weighted by the test maker. Some students find value in predicting the questions and learning specific answers to those questions. Be alert, however, to the possibility that the actual test might represent a radical departure from your prediction. This caution underscores the importance of learning underlying concepts.

1.5 BECOME FAMILIAR WITH THE TEST'S PURPOSE AND FORMAT IN ADVANCE

Gaining familiarity with the test's purpose and format can help you in two ways: First, you will be able to focus your time and energy upon the particular aspect of a subject on which you will be tested. For example, if the purpose of a test is to measure your knowledge of eighteenth century English writers, then you can concentrate on that topic. Second, if the format of a standardized test is ascertained in advance, then you will know which types of test items to study. For example, if the test includes word analogies, number series, reading comprehension, and vocabulary items, you would know that your time would be best spent studying the chapters of this book in which these types of items are discussed. (See also principle 4.1.)

THE OK4R METHOD OF READING[1]

Before

O   1. *Overview.* Take about five minutes to read introductory and summary paragraphs of the assignment. Then read center and side headings, or topic sentences if there are no headings, to determine general content and sequence of topics. Locate the main divisions.

[1] Taken from *How to Study in College*, a paperback by Walter Pauk, Houghton Mifflin Company, Boston, 1962. Reprinted by permission of both author and publisher.

K 2. *Key Ideas.* Distinguish key ideas from secondary ideas and supporting materials. Convert headings or topic sentences into questions—a sure way to become involved in the author's ideas.

During

R¹ 3. *Read.* Read the sections or paragraphs consecutively to answer your questions and to see *how* supporting materials clarify or prove key points. Pay close attention to transitional words and phrases. If you are reading persuasive material, keep asking yourself: What is the evidence? Does it prove the point? Is there enough support? Do I believe this? Why or why not? If you are reading exposition, ask yourself the following questions: What is the main point in this section? Does this example make the main point clear? How? Can I think of other examples?

R² 4. *Recall.* After reading, test your memory and understanding. Without looking at the book, try to say or write the main points and supporting materials in your own words. If you cannot do so immediately after reading, you cannot hope to tomorrow in class or next week in an exam. Now—but not before—take brief summary notes in your notebook or underline key points in your book and make "recall" notes in the margins. Remember to *understand first*, then write.

After

R³ 5. *Reflect.* Step 4, Recall, will help fix the material in your mind. To make it really yours, go further: Think about it. Relating new facts and ideas to others you already know gives added meaning to new and old knowledge and establishes both more firmly in your mind. This is the essence of all creative thinking: the discovery of new relationships and new significance.

R⁴ 6. *Review.* To keep material fresh in mind, review it periodically. Reread your notes and say over the sequence of main ideas and supporting materials until you have them once more firmly in mind. Mastery is a never-ending process.

THE NOTE–TAKING TECHNIQUE

The paper on which the notes are to be taken should be ruled to look like this:

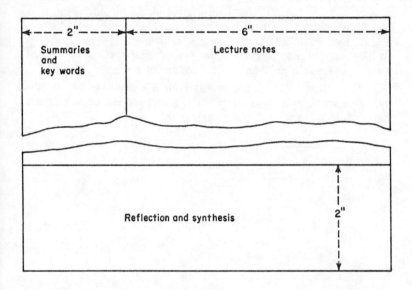

This format provides the perfect opportunity for following through with the 5 Rs of note-taking. Here they are:

1. *Record.* During the lecture, record in the 6-inch column as many meaningful facts and ideas as you can.

2. *Reduce.* As soon after as possible, summarize these ideas and facts concisely in the 2-inch column. Summarizing clarifies meanings and relationships, reinforces continuity, and strengthens memory. Also it is a way of preparing for examinations graduaⅼⅼy and well ahead of time.

3. *Recite.* Now cover the 6-inch column. Using only your jottings in the 2-inch column as clues or "flags" to help you recall, say over the facts and ideas of the lecture as fully as you can, not by rote, but in your own words and with as much appreciation of the meaning as you can. Then, uncovering the notes, verify what you have said. This procedure is the most powerful study technique known to psychologists.

4. *Reflect.* Professor Hans Bethe, prominent nuclear physicist at Cornell University, has said that a student who goes only as far as his textbooks and lectures take him can become proficient, but never creative. Creativity, even real mastery of a subject, comes only with reflection. Seeing new material in the light of what you already know is the only road to original ideas, for having an idea is nothing more than discovering a relationship not seen before. And it is impossible to have ideas without reflecting—i.e., thinking. So that you do not forget the results of your reflections, record them in the space provided at the bottom of the sheet.

5. *Review.* If you will repeat Step 3 every week or so, you will retain most of what you have learned, and you will be able to use your knowledge to greater and greater effect.

THE NOTE–TAKING TECHNIQUE[1]
(*Illustrated*)

American Philosophy–333 – Sept. 23, 1969 – Prof. Murphy

Man's phil–way he looks at life–based on daily experience	1. What Am. Phil. is & what part it plays in Am. culture.
Phil–Truth– based on principles.	a. Man's phil.–way he looks at and evaluates the world.
Definite relationship bet. culture & phil.	b. Philosophy–pursuit of truth–attempt to investigate reason or justification for our ultimate beliefs–push reason back as far as possible, until we get at self-evident truths. See Collingwood on presuppositions.
1. culture insecure	c. Ultimate beliefs are usually the influence of our times. As ideas chg., the traditional ideas are challenged. When challenges arise, then philosophies appear to find some fundamental truth––to bring truth into focus. Examine, adjust, throw out, chg. current thinking & beliefs.
2. tensions arise	
3. questions asked	
4. phil. answers	
Opinions of market-place influence people.	d. Climate of beliefs: these are beliefs people hold without inquiry or investigation
	Assignment: Jonathan Edwards for Fri. 1st five selections – last & important. Sup'l: H. Schneider, Hist. Am. Phil.
Edwards–Calvinist predeterminism	2. Jonathan Edwards–Calvinist theologian
	a. Doctrine: absolute sovereignty of God––will–motion are predetermined by God. Look up predestination.
Is there Free Will?	b. People started to think about Free will. If God does everything, what can the human will do? Nothing? Conflict!
To conserve est. faith, Edwards gave basic reasons for faith.	c. Edwards–conservative–wanted to justify the established faith & bring into relation with current thought.
	— — felt the need of giving reasons for beliefs.
	— — didn't simply say, "This is revealed."
	Example: When Jefferson severed connections with Britain, he gave reasons based on self-evident truths.

A country does not necessarily develop its culture according to an *a priori* set of philosophical principles ; more likely, the culture develops first, then philosophical principles are brought forth to support the culture. Furthermore, as the culture grows and changes, so do the philosophical principles which support it.

---

[1] The discussion on note-taking as well as the above example were taken from *How to Study in College*, a paperback by Walter Pauk, Houghton Mifflin Company, Boston, 1962. Reprinted by permission of both author and publisher.

2.

EMOTIONAL AND PHYSICAL PREPARATION

"Knowing your stuff," though an absolutely necessary condition, is not the complete answer for doing well on examinations. If you are to make optimum use of the "stuff" you know, attitudes and behaviors must be taken into consideration.

2.1 REALIZE WHO IS ON YOUR SIDE

Above all, guard against feelings of resentment or anger toward the test administrator. He will be trying to help you do your best by keeping noise at a minimum, seeing that the temperature and light are right, supplying you with extra pencils, answering what questions that he can about the test, and the like.

Guard, also, against thinking that certain teachers always give unfair tests or mark them unfairly. This attitude is usually adopted by poor students who strangely enough fear a fair examination. They feel that a fair examination would show up their weaknesses, whereas an unfair one can be offered as an excuse for doing poorly.

2.2 APPRECIATE THE USEFULNESS OF TESTS

Knowing that tests perform important functions may help to motivate you to work hard preparing for and taking them. Their primary purpose is to provide a scale to measure knowledge and capabilities. It is important that a correct assessment of your abilities be made, since many people will make use of your scores. Teachers and school personnel use the scores not only to assign grades, but more importantly to determine future courses and programs of study. Test scores and scholastic grades are also used by college admissions officers, scholarship committees, and employment managers. Not to be overlooked, either, are their benefits to you. If the tests are validly measuring what they should, the scores can give you some idea of your competence and aptitude, and thus guide you in selecting future courses and direct you in planning your career.

To do less well on a test than you are capable of doing distorts the measurement of your achievement and aptitude for those who may refer to your test scores. Worst of all, to do less than you are capable of doing is unfair to yourself.

2.3 RELAX

Keep calm, especially before the examination. Some tension is natural and serves to keep you mentally and physically alert, but too much tension may bring about mental blocking. Blocking usually leads to frustration, worry, and more tension which, in turn, may bring on more blocking, thus compounding the difficulty.

One way to avoid accumulating excess tension is to anticipate your needs. Don't be in a rush. Allow plenty of time to accomplish all the things you have to do before the test. Gather the materials you will need (such as eraser, pen, notebook) the night before to help ensure a smooth start.

Once in the examination room you can keep tension under control by concentrating on some points you wish to remember. Bring important notebooks or textbooks (or even this book) with you for this purpose. Once the examination begins, record on the back of a teacher-made examination ideas and facts you have memorized which you fear you may forget. Exclude thoughts of failure by focusing on the examination itself.

2.4 BE PREPARED FOR A "FIGHT"

Do not go into the testing room with a negative attitude of "I'm sure I won't pass," or even a neutral attitude of "Let the chips fall where they may." To do your best, you must think positively. On the other hand, an *overconfident* attitude may keep you from being as alert as you might be. Also, if your guard is down and you encounter a test which is much more difficult than anticipated, your chances of being overwhelmed are increased.

Don't believe that the only questions you are capable of answering correctly are those you know right away. By working hard you can often raise your score considerably. That you really know more than you think you do and get credit for on a test is proved time and time again when the test answers are discussed in class. Through persistence and the use of the principles discussed in this book you can overcome the tendency to underachieve on tests. Remember, always work hard throughout the full time allowed. Don't come into the examination room with thoughts of leaving early or doing anything less than your best. Stick to the job!

2.5 CONCENTRATE

Avoid distractions. Once in the examination room, do not be distracted by studying for another course. This can interfere with the material you need to know for the present examination. Before the examination begins, preoccupy yourself by going over in your mind the material which you studied as preparation. Then when the exam begins, think only about the examination, that is, reading and compre-

hending the questions, and formulating and writing answers.
To eliminate other potential sources of distraction during an
examination, do not sit near a window if you can help it, or
friends, or attractive classmates.

2.6 WEIGH LOSSES AGAINST GAINS BEFORE ALTERING YOUR PHYSICAL SELF

It is generally accepted that good physical condition enables
a student to concentrate better. Yet, many students endan-
ger this by doing one or more of the following: first, subject-
ing themselves to drastic losses of sleep by cramming for
exams; second, taking sleeping pills and tranquilizers; and
third, taking pep pills.

Our personal stand is a Spartan one: Rely on your
natural self. Don't use a crutch. But there are extenuating
circumstances, and for these we suggest weighing the prob-
able losses against the expected gains.

  a. *Cramming and loss of sleep.* Is the gain in informa-
     tion worth the sacrifice in effectiveness during the
     examination? The answer depends on whether the
     exam is to be factual or thought provoking. For ex-
     ample, the *Scholastic Aptitude Test* (SAT), which
     requires thought and analysis, can be handled much
     better after a good night's sleep, than after any
     amount of cramming.
  b. *Sleeping pills and tranquilizers.* Is the gain in addi-
     tional relaxation and easing of tension during the
     examination worth the danger of the loss of alertness
     and motivation?
  c. *Pep pills.* Is the gain in alertness and added stimula-
     tion worth the potential loss of the ability to think
     through and concentrate on thought-provoking prob-
     lems?

PART 2

PRINCIPLES
OF TAKING
ANY
EXAMINATION

No matter what kind of test you are taking, there are some general rules which you should always follow. You should use your time wisely, and you should read test directions and test questions carefully to avoid needless errors. In addition, there are some guidelines concerning how to "reason out" the correct answers to questions; the chapters in this part of the book will introduce you to the principles discussing these rules and guidelines. Because the principles are applicable to all examinations, they are especially important. You should understand them fully.

Although some principles may be generally helpful for many kinds of tests, they may also be especially helpful in only one kind or at the most several kinds of tests. To avoid undue repetition, the test-taking principles have been listed but once under the kind of test for which they are particularly helpful.

**USING
TIME
WISELY**

Almost all tests have a time limit. Some tests are essentially *power* tests; that is, you will have a liberal amount of time to complete them. Other tests are essentially *speed* tests; that is, you will have to work quickly and make optimum use of your time if you desire to complete all the questions or do well. With all tests you should be especially aware of the time allowed and remember to pace yourself accordingly.

3.1 KNOW HOW LONG YOU HAVE TO COMPLETE THE TEST

Make a mental note of the number of minutes you are allowed to work on the test questions; if you have any doubt, ask the examiner. On standardized tests, the time allowed is frequently indicated on the direction page.

3.2 LOOK OVER THE ENTIRE TEST BEFORE YOU START TO ANSWER ANY QUESTIONS

It is obviously impossible to know how fast to answer the questions if you are not aware of how many and what type of questions there are to answer. Only by looking over the entire test and getting an idea of its scope will you know how fast you must work through the items. The minute you spend in surveying will help you make better use of time and thereby improve your test performance.

3.3 SET UP A SCHEDULE FOR PROGRESS THROUGH TEACHER-MADE TESTS

Determine how far you should be at the end of a specified number of minutes. This should not be too difficult if you know the total number of minutes in which you have to complete the test, and the number and types of questions. In setting up this schedule, leave some time at the end to go back to complete any skipped items and to check some completed items. Items which need more time to answer, which count more points, and which are more difficult to answer (such as essay questions) should, in most cases, be apportioned more time.

The practice situations for setting up a schedule found on page 20 will provide you with some experience in constructing guideposts to help pace yourself.

Periodically check on your progress to maintain proper speed. What good is a schedule if you don't check to see whether or not you are keeping to it? You should wear a watch to the examination unless you are sure the room has a clock which can be seen easily.

Setting up a time schedule on *standardized tests* is *not* necessary. On standardized tests the more difficult items are usually placed last. Do not be so concerned with finishing as with moving along at the fastest rate at which you can function well. The main idea on standardized tests is to get as many items right as possible.

3.4 BEGIN TO WORK AS RAPIDLY AS POSSIBLE WITH REASONABLE ASSURANCE OF ACCURACY

Just as a fast start is necessary for a track runner, so is a good start important when taking a test. Do not waste time getting settled. Have your paper and pencils and your mental framework all set to go before the test begins. If directions are given before the timed portion of the test is begun (as in many standardized tests), be sure you understand them ahead of time. One leading authority on the College Board tests said that the outstanding fault of those who did poorly on these tests was their wasting valuable time at the start of each examination by going back to reread directions with which they should have been thoroughly familiar before the test began.

3.5 OMIT OR GUESS AT ITEMS WHICH STUMP YOU

This principle is essentially the same as the familiar rule not to spend too much time on any one item. If you do spend too much time, chances are you will not be able to stick to your schedule and will not be able to devote the desired amount of time you have scheduled for the other questions.

If the test is primarily one of speed and you seriously doubt that you will have time to reconsider an item later, then make a guess and go on to the other questions; it is a good practice to check items which could use further consideration, or items which have been skipped.

You should avoid skipping too many items. It takes time to read the items over again and to repeat the thinking processes necessary for comprehension. If you do find time to get back to an item, concentrate on it and make the best answer you can.

3.6 WORK FAST ON THOSE ITEMS WHICH WILL YIELD THE MOST POINTS IN A GIVEN AMOUNT OF TIME

Unless instructed otherwise, get the most points in the shortest time possible. This principle implies that for tests consisting of relatively few essays or problems you should answer the easiest questions first. When a test consists of a large number of objective items, it is usually best to work the items in sequence; this is especially advisable with standardized tests which usually arrange the items from easy to difficult.

3.7 USE THE TIME REMAINING AFTER COMPLETION OF THE TEST TO RECONSIDER AND IMPROVE YOUR ANSWERS

Stay in the examination room for the full time allotted. Do not give up; there is evidence that persistence pays off with higher scores. The first one to walk out of the room often mistakenly believes his early departure will impress the others. Such a student is misguided. He often pays a high price for a brief "moment of glory."

If time permits, check all your answers. Do not be afraid to change answers if it seems desirable. Contrary to popular belief, research studies have shown that test takers generally increase their scores with changes. When changing an answer, however, make sure you have taken into consideration the reasons why you originally answered as you did.

PROBLEMS FOR PRACTICE

Setting Up a Time Schedule for Progress through Teacher-made Tests

To gain the maximum benefit from each of the following practice situations, we suggest that you calculate how much time you would allocate to the various portions of each test. After you have made your calculation for one practice situation, check to see how your time strategy compares with our suggested guidelines; then go on to the next situation.

Situation 1 The test consists of forty true-false questions. You have twenty minutes to complete the test.

Suggested Guideline This obviously is a highly speeded test. Answer the questions as fast as you can, consistent with accuracy. Do not expect to have time left over to reconsider many of your answers.

Situation 2 The test consists of four essay questions. You have forty minutes to complete the test.

Suggested Guideline Allowing some time to read over your answers and make changes, you can spend somewhat less than ten minutes on each question.

Situation 3 The test consists of thirty multiple-choice questions. You have fifty minutes to complete the test. The test starts at 2:00.

Suggested Guideline You should allow some time (say, ten minutes) to go back to skipped items and to check your answers. That leaves thirty questions in forty minutes, or about fifteen questions in twenty minutes, or about eight questions every ten minutes. If you skip a large number of items, you should increase your pace; if you answer all the items as you go, you can afford to slow down a bit. In any event, by 2:25 you should have answered at least half the questions.

Situation 4 The test consists of forty-five multiple-choice questions and two essay questions worth 20 percent each. You have one and a half hours to complete the test.

Suggested Guideline Allowing fifteen minutes to check your answers and complete those you skip, that leaves seventy-five minutes to divide between the two types of questions. It would be desirable to allot 40 percent of the seventy-five minutes (that is, thirty minutes) for the two essays and forty-five minutes ($75 - 30 = 45$) for the objective items. At that rate you must complete one multiple-choice question per minute. After fifteen minutes you should have attempted fifteen such questions; after thirty minutes, thirty; and after forty-five minutes, all. After one hour, you should have answered the first essay and after one and a quarter hours you should have attempted all the questions.

Situation 5 The test consists of twenty short-answer questions and four problems. You figure the four problems will take somewhat more than half your time. You have two hours to complete the test.

Suggested Guideline Allowing twenty minutes or so for checking and going back to omitted items, you are left with one hundred minutes to divide between the two types. It would be desirable if you could allot sixty of the one hundred minutes for the problems and forty minutes for the short-answer questions. In other words, you would have to answer the short-answer questions at the rate of one every two minutes and the problems at the rate of one every fifteen minutes.

4.

**READING
DIRECTIONS AND
QUESTIONS
CAREFULLY**

Testing involves precise communication between test maker and test taker. The test maker, in carefully worded directions and questions, tries to find out the extent of the test taker's understanding, knowledge, and skill in certain areas. You, the test taker, try to show (tell) what you know by choosing correct options and writing skillful answers.

The test taker's task is twofold. First, you must be able to understand with precision what the test maker wants; second, you must be able to communicate what you know. The second task will be dealt with later in this book; the first task, that of understanding what the test maker wants, will be the focus of this chapter.

Students tend to place too little emphasis on the necessity for carefully reading directions and questions. A perfectly "correct" and well-written answer to a question *not* asked will receive no credit. Frequently, understanding what is wanted—understanding the question—may be more difficult than the idea or concept being tested for. Surely it makes good sense to look at the question before you leap into an answer.

Research conducted at the University of Chicago determined that the most distinguishing characteristic of poor test takers was their tendency to *mis*read directions and questions. Answers were often "off target" because these students jumped to conclusions about what was being asked. The sad part was that many points which should have been earned were lost even though these students really knew the material. The principles in this chapter will help you to understand the message which the test maker is trying to communicate in his directions and questions. Once you understand this message, you can get credit for what you know.

4.1 BECOME FAMILIAR WITH TEST DIRECTIONS AHEAD OF TIME

Information about the types of questions in many standardized tests (such as those taken in connection with college and job applications) is frequently available to the prospective test taker. It is tremendously important to become thoroughly familiar with these descriptive and illustrative materials well in advance of the actual test. A thorough understanding of the types of questions which you will encounter on the test will not only save time but also prevent misunderstanding what you are to do. Such misunderstandings are most likely to occur on important tests which often carry directions somewhat out of the ordinary.

The College Entrance Examination Board publishes a booklet called "A Description of the College Board Scholastic Aptitude Test."[1] Any student who does not read this booklet thoroughly will be at a disadvantage when compared with other students taking the same examination who have read the booklet.

Many teachers make available copies of old examinations. Seize this opportunity to acquaint yourself with the special kinds of directions and questions each teacher is likely to use (review principle 1.5).

A word of warning: It is important that you do not assume that the same directions will appear on similar tests.

[1] College Entrance Examination Board, Publications Order Office, Box 592, Princeton, New Jersey 08540 (*free*).

Always read directions carefully to make sure that some changes have not been inserted.

There will be times when you won't be able to study a test's directions in advance. But when it is possible, we repeat, you should become familiar with them to save time and prevent errors.

4.2 PAY PARTICULAR ATTENTION TO THOSE PARTS OF THE DIRECTIONS WHICH MOST INFLUENCE HOW YOU WILL TAKE THE TEST.

The directions provide the information you need to make good decisions concerning which questions to answer, what kind of answer to make, how fast to work, and so forth. Below is a list of important points you should look for when reading directions.

a. *Time limit.* The time you are permitted to spend taking the test will guide you in determining how fast you should go through the questions and how complete your answers should be. Knowing how much time you have is necessary for setting up a schedule for progress through teacher-made tests.

b. *Aids.* Are textbooks, notes, slide rules, scrap paper, or other aids permitted? Be sure you know what you can and cannot use.

c. *Order of answering.* Is there a special order in which you must answer the items? If so, follow this order, not only because you may be penalized if you do not, but also because you are most likely to do your best when you take the test in the manner planned. If there is no restriction about the order in which you must answer the items, work first on those items which will yield the most points in a given amount of time.

d. *Number of questions you must answer.* Do you have to answer all the questions, or are you permitted a choice? If you do *not* have to answer every question, it is foolish to waste time answering questions that will not count toward your score.

e. *Type of answer required.* Do the directions specify what kind of answers you should give and what form they should be in? Are calculations and other preliminary steps required, or only the answer? Is the maximum number of words you can use in writing your answer specified? Are you supposed to circle, cross out, or mark on an answer sheet the correct answer? Do you have to copy the question over as part of your answer? (Do not, unless you have to. It takes valuable time.) For true-false statements, do you have to correct the false statements? On matching items, may words in the answer list be used more than once? These are just a few of the many possible kinds of directions; look for them, and follow them precisely.

f. *Scoring.* Whenever possible, try to determine ahead of time how the test will be scored. This will aid you in planning the distribution of your time; you will probably spend more time on questions that count most.

Another reason for determining how the questions will be scored is that this knowledge will help you decide whether or not to guess. Although principle 8.11 provides in some detail a strategy for guessing, it is worth mentioning that unless you know how many points you will be penalized for an incorrect answer you cannot make an intelligent decision whether or not to guess.

4.3 TAKE THE PRACTICE QUESTIONS SERIOUSLY

At the beginning of many tests you will find an exercise or two to practice on. The correct answers are usually given. These exercises give you a chance to make sure that you and the test maker are communicating. If you do not understand the directions, you may find this out when you attempt the practice questions; so do not peek ahead to see what the given answer is.

If there is an explanation of why a particular answer is correct, study this explanation. Even though you may have answered the question correctly, a study of the test maker's reasons will often help you in thinking through other, more difficult questions.

Another reason for seriously attempting the problems for practice is that they give you a running start; that is, they place you in an appropriate thinking groove. When the actual test begins, you won't have to overcome inertia.

4.4 KEEP THE DIRECTIONS IN MIND WHEN ANSWERING THE TEST ITEMS

Often the instructions direct you to choose an *incorrect* answer from among several correct ones. For example,

> *A famous English playwright:*
>   *a)   Christopher Marlowe*
>   *b)   William Shakespeare*
>   *c)   William Congreve*
>   *d)   Washington Irving*

This item appeared on a test in which the directions were: "Each of the following items contains three correct and one incorrect answer. Choose the incorrect answer." Because Marlowe, Shakespeare, and Congreve were all English playwrights the correct option is Washington Irving. William Shakespeare will be chosen by the student who does not keep the directions in mind when answering the questions.

Consider this item:

> *Cream is heavier than milk.*
> *Cream is found at the bottom of a quart of milk that is*
>   *not homogenized. (True or False)*

A student who answers this question without first carefully reading the instructions that accompany it will be in trouble because the directions state that he is to *assume* the first statement is *true* and then to judge whether or not the second statement would be true on the basis of the first. With this set of directions, you can see that the proper answer is *true*. If cream *were* heavier than milk (and you are told to assume that it is), then cream would indeed be at the bottom of a quart of milk. This type of test item is used to measure reasoning ability, not factual knowledge.

The moral of these two examples is: Do *not* depend upon the questions in the test to tell you the nature of the directions.

4.5 ASK THE EXAMINER FOR CLARIFICATION WHEN NECESSARY

If it is permitted, ask for help (when you need it) to understand the directions of a test. It is important to understand the directions before you begin the test. Even for most standardized tests, the examiner is permitted to help you understand the directions.

On most standardized tests the examiner is instructed not to help students with the questions themselves; this is stipulated so that no student will receive special help from an overly kind proctor. The directions, in such a case, will include something like this: "Once the test begins do not ask any questions." If the test is in progress, it is better that you spend your time trying to figure out for yourself what is being asked rather than wait for the examiner to come to your seat and tell you he cannot help you. Of course, it is a different matter if your question concerns the mechanics of taking the test, such as where to record an answer or where to sharpen your pencil.

There is no rule that a teacher cannot help interpret questions on his own classroom tests. You should realize that no matter how experienced the teacher is as a test maker, it is still likely that he will construct ambiguous items. It is very reasonable for you to ask such questions as: Would you define this word for me; should we interpret this to mean such and such; and when you consider this question from this point of view, the answer would be this, but under such and such a condition the answer would now be this—which do you mean?

Remember, the worst the teacher can do is refuse to answer. Even in that case, you've lost little, if anything. In fact, if the teacher listens to your questions and will not help, it may suggest that he feels you do *not* have a valid point; perhaps you should reconsider your question and the item.

4.6 BE ALERT TO READ THE QUESTIONS AS THEY ARE, NOT AS YOU WOULD LIKE THEM TO BE

We frequently see what we want to see. When you encounter an easy, familiar-looking item, don't jump to the conclusion that you know what it is. Read the question carefully to make sure it is indeed the same question you thought it was. Many good teachers will test for a point which was emphasized in class or in the textbook but in a slightly different way. Changing just one word in a question can alter the answer; read every word.

4.7 PAY ATTENTION TO THE KEY TERMS IN THE QUESTIONS

Every word in a question is important. If you mistakenly read *ounces* for *pounds* or overlook a *not*, you will answer the question incorrectly. Such errors involve carelessness and can be reduced by more alert reading.

We have all experienced missing test questions we should have answered correctly because of such careless errors. But for each question missed because of *misreading* there are several other questions answered incorrectly because of *misinterpretation*. We consider those words upon which a precise and accurate interpretation of the question asked and the desired response depend to be "key terms."

Circle the key terms in this example taken from a standardized test in American history.

Show two different ways in which democracy was extended during the Jacksonian period.

We did *not* circle the words *two* and *Jacksonian.* Like most words which are underlined or italicized or relate to proper names, *two* and *Jacksonian* are important words and to misread them would be unfortunate, but there is nothing subtle about these terms; there is little interpretation involved.

We did, however, consider *show* to be a key term in the question above. Demonstration with evidence and not just description is required. Many key terms of procedure, direction, quantity, and degree are listed, defined, and discussed in Appendix I. Look over Appendix I before proceeding with the rest of this chapter to see how it can help you. *The care we took in writing this appendix is indicative of the importance we place on key words.*

Another type of key term is illustrated in the above example by the word *extended.* This word signifies that the answer should contain evidence of how democracy was increased and not just how it was preserved.

Circle the key terms in the introductory line of this multiple-choice question:

The outbreak of World War I was a direct result of the
   a)   sinking of the Lusitania
   b)   assassination of the heir to the throne of Austria-Hungary
   c)   rise of nationalism in Europe.
   d)   imperialism of England and France and the subsequent jealousy of Germany
   e)   attack on Pearl Harbor

If you circled *World War I* or just the *I,* you identified an important word, because to read *II* for *I* could have led you to choose (e), the wrong answer. We circled the term *direct* (or *direct result*) because keen interpretation is involved with this term. Options (c) and (d) are clearly underlying causes of World War I, but *direct* alerts us to look for an immediate activator—a triggering event.

The important point is *not* whether you are able to distinguish as we do between key terms and other important words, rather it is whether you are able to interpret all the words accurately so that you will know exactly what is being asked.

4.8 USE ANY REMAINING TIME AFTER YOU COMPLETE THE TEST TO CHECK YOUR INTERPRETATION OF DIRECTIONS AND QUESTIONS

Although similar to principle 3.7, this principle emphasizes checking your *interpretation* of both the directions and the questions. Many open-ended questions (e.g., essay questions) contain several subquestions, and it is these questions and complicated directions which are most likely to be misinterpreted.

The practice problems at the end of this chapter will give you a chance to apply some of the eight principles just presented. Answer the questions and check your answers.

PROBLEMS FOR PRACTICE

Questions

Multiple-choice Items. Some of the items below may have more than one correct answer. Circle the letters preceding all the correct options.

1. Which city is not a capital of a state?
   a) Buffalo b) Miami c) Harrisburg d) Lansing

2. A four-legged animal:
   a) rose b) house c) pigeon d) ratel

Open-ended Items.

3. Who are the members of the American cabinet, and how are they chosen?

4. A small flag is shaped like an isosceles triangle 5 inches high and 12 inches long. How many square yards of material were needed to make the flag?

Answers

Did you notice in the directions that there could be more than one correct answer? You probably did, but could there be an item in which no option was correct? Best to check on this. The directions are not clear.

1. A key word in this question is *not*. It makes options (a) and (b) the correct ones.

2. Did you misread *horse* for *house*? Did you incorrectly check *pigeon* as a four-legged animal? If there must be at least one correct answer, you could have arrived at the correct answer (d) by elimination.

3. Careful, this is really two questions in one; many open-ended questions, including essay questions, are really several questions in one. To get full credit, you must answer all the parts. In this example, you must both list the members of the cabinet and tell how they are chosen. It is not entirely clear whether the test maker wants the titles of the cabinet members (e.g., Secretary of the Treasury) or the names of the present members, or both. Best to check on this.

The second *are* in question 3 is a clue to the question's intention. "How *are* they chosen" should mean "How are the positions filled," whereas "How were they chosen" would probably mean here "How were these particular individuals chosen." Further examples of how the structure or context of a sentence can be helpful in determining the type of answer you should give are discussed in principles 7.3 and 12.4.

4. Another ambiguous question. Cloth does not come in triangular shapes. But if the question is part of a mathematics examination (rather than one in home economics), it is obvious that the question is asking for the area of the

triangle. Do not be cute and answer, "depends on the width of the material."

Do you know which of the two shapes shown to the right is intended? Does it matter? Did you notice that the flag was isosceles in shape? You need to know this in order to solve the problem.

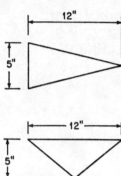

Did you notice the answer requested is to be in square yards? Figure the area in square inches and change to square yards, or change inches to yards and calculate the area. Do it both ways as a check—if you have the time.

5.

USING GOOD
REASONING
TECHNIQUES[1]

As indicated in principle 2.4, there are many questions or parts of questions which you can answer correctly if you are willing to work at them. In this chapter we shall suggest ways to help you "reason out" what the correct answers to problems should be. Some reasoning techniques peculiar to objective tests and numerical problems are reserved for Chapters 8 and 14; now we shall concentrate on methods appropriate for a wide variety of test items.

Naturally, problem-solving techniques cannot serve as a substitute for the basic knowledge of subject matter or for certain types of ability. Nevertheless, you can often reason out an answer, even with a limited background. Reasoning is important.

5.1 MAKE A SINCERE ATTEMPT AT EVERY QUESTION

Do not avoid questions that *look* complicated and involved. One research study showed that the willingness of test-wise

[1] Much of the material presented in this chapter is adapted from Benjamin S. Bloom and Lois J. Broder, *Problem-Solving Processes of College Students: An Exploratory Investigation*, The University of Chicago Press, Chicago, 1950.

students to tackle longer questions was one of the factors which differentiated them from students *not* so sophisticated. Don't give up on questions which seem to require extracurricular knowledge or which contain references to things that seem unfamiliar to you. These things may be unessential for determining an acceptable answer. You may be able to figure out the answer anyway.

Of course, it is usually foolish to spend too much time on any one question (principle 3.5). If you do not seem to be making any progress, try another question (principle 5.6). But before you give up, satisfy yourself that you have made a sincere attempt to figure out an answer to the question.

5.2 THINK THROUGH THE QUESTIONS

The emphasis of this principle is on the word *think*. Think— use your head—to obtain an acceptable answer. Do not be satisfied to rely on your impressions or feelings unless you have to or are told to do so. Think through each problem on the basis of what is stated in the question; do not merely put down a suitable-sounding answer you remember from your textbook, class notes, etc. The answer to a similar, but not identical, question may be misleading and incorrect. (Trying to remember an approach you used to answer a similar question can be helpful.)

Think about the question at hand. If the question is about naval battles, do not start thinking about fun at the beach; control these irrelevant free associations.

5.3 BE AGGRESSIVE IN YOUR ATTEMPT TO ANSWER QUESTIONS

Interrogate yourself. Keep asking yourself questions like: What is the question I am trying to answer? What are the key terms? What is my best guess on the meaning of this unfamiliar word? What are the elements or parts of the problem? What are the concepts that apply in this case? What does my own experience tell me that might help in answering the question? Are the instances from my experience relevant? What kind of answer is needed here? Can I break the question down or translate it in some way to make it easier to answer? (Suggestions related to the last question are discussed in the next principle.)

5.4 TRANSLATE MATERIAL IN A QUESTION TO A DIFFERENT FORM

Do not expect that by just looking at a question the answer is going to pop up. It is sometimes helpful to change the problem into language which is easier to handle. For example, make the question more concrete. In a numerical problem, this might mean substituting numbers for abstract ideas or symbols; in a history problem, it might be advantageous to change dates to events. Long and involved problems can profitably be broken down into parts, and by working to find the answers to these smaller parts, you will be able to answer the entire question. (Principle 14.2 contains additional techniques and examples.)

5.5 EVALUATE YOUR ANSWER

Does your answer deal with the question asked? Is it the kind of answer you think is needed (see principle 5.3)? Have you, by translating materials as suggested in principle 5.4, changed the question and thus come up with an inappropriate answer? Be sure that the alternative you have selected or the essay you have written is pertinent to the question.

5.6 IF STUCK, GO ON TO ANOTHER QUESTION

This principle is not really in conflict with the previous ones mentioned in this chapter, which, basically, advised you not to give up too quickly but to do your utmost to work out the answer. But when you have tried the procedures mentioned here and when you have tried attacking the question from a variety of approaches without success, go on to another question.

Going on to another question has merit not only because you might be wasting valuable time that could be better spent on other questions, but also because "changing the scene" helps to free your mind from any blocking that may have made you forget important material. Even while you are working on another problem, the question which resisted solution often remains suspended in your mind, ready for you to reattempt a solution which may be suggested by other questions.

PART 3

PRINCIPLES OF ANSWERING SPECIAL TYPES OF TEST ITEMS

The questions which make up most achievement and aptitude tests are really based on just a few basic types. These types are: the essay, the sentence completion, the objective test item, the verbal analogy, the number series, and the configuration series. In this part of the book a separate chapter is devoted to each of these types.

**ESSAY
QUESTIONS**

An essay question requires the test taker to compose his own answer, which may vary in length from a mere sentence or two to a lengthy discourse. And the content of the answer may vary from the mere recall of a specific bit of information to a well-organized, critical evaluation of a philosophical position.

The ideal answer should show that you (a) understand the question, (b) know the relevant material, (c) can present the material in an organized manner, and (d) can present your ideas clearly. The objective of this chapter is to help you write such answers.

6.1 REMEMBER THE GENERAL PRINCIPLES OF TEST-TAKING

Review and keep in mind all the principles put forth in Chapters 1 through 5. In addition to your review, go over the highlights, below, of some of the previously stated principles which have a direct bearing on essay questions.

   a. *Be prepared.* There is no substitute for "knowing your stuff." No amount of test-taking technique can make up for a deficiency in knowledge. No amount of proficiency in stating, developing, and evaluating ideas can take the place of facts.

After you learn the "raw" facts and ideas, together with their supporting material, we suggest that you finish off your studying for essay examinations by testing yourself for flexibility. To do this, turn to Appendix I, and subject yourself to questions which you can form on the basis of the key words and terms appearing in the various clusters. For example, by looking at your notes, choose several of the outstanding ideas, and then try to *compare, contrast, differentiate, analyze, relate, criticize, evaluate,* and *interpret* them.

b. *Record on the back of a teacher-made examination some facts and formulas you have memorized.* Do this even before you read the questions. This suggestion, mentioned in principle 2.3, helps prevent blocking and inertia. The minute that it takes to jot down a few facts is usually a good investment.

If, however, you are taking a standardized test, you may be instructed *not* to write or make calculations except in a designated area on the examination paper. In such cases, you should comply with the directions.

c. *Read the question carefully.* One of the most common comments on returned examination papers, often written in bold handwriting to show the instructor's emphasis and impatience, is *"Read the question!!"* Make sure you understand what is being asked before you begin to write your answer. Answer exactly what the instructor intended.

To be sure you do, circle key words and terms (see principle 4.7 and Appendix I). Do not write a three-page answer if only a paragraph, or even a sentence, is requested. Many essay questions contain several parts or subquestions; be sure to address your answer to all of them!

d. *Try hard.* If you find that you are unprepared to answer most of the questions, do not give up or make a half-hearted attempt. Instead, work harder than ordinarily to put together an outline of plausible ideas; then, write neatly and forcefully. It is often surprising to see the string of ideas you can pull out of your mind once you catch hold of even one idea, however fragmentary.

e. *Use time wisely.* It is easy to lose track of time when you are answering a question on a topic about which you know a great deal. Allocate your time among the questions, saving more time for essay questions which carry greater weight and require longer answers.

If you do have some time remaining, read over your answers. Frequently you can add some additional ideas which may come to mind. At the very least, you can correct misspellings or insert words to clarify an idea.

6.2 READ ALL THE ESSAY ITEMS, JOTTING DOWN BESIDE EACH QUESTION THE POINTS THAT OCCUR TO YOU

By following this principle *before you begin writing your answers*, you will have a chance to unburden your mind of those fresh, important first impressions.

There are several reasons why this time will be well spent. First, by reading all the questions at the start you will have a chance to think over some of them, perhaps subconsciously, while answering others. Second, because your mind follows chains of associations, ideas you have at the start of an examination may be lost if you don't write them down. The effort expended in answering one question in depth can block out ideas pertaining to another question. Third, the points you write down can serve as the beginning of an outline for your answers.

At this point, work fast. Do not linger over any questions waiting for additional ideas. However, do not jot down your ideas so sketchily that when you come back you cannot reconstruct them.

Here is an example of an essay question with key terms circled and marginal notes (based on immediate recall) recorded.

Competition bet. countries led to nationalism

No need for other countries for trade

Minerals (coffee, spices etc)
Wanted money & land
War.

Cortez & Aztecs

The fifteenth- and sixteenth-century voyages of exploration produced lasting changes in the political and social structure of Western Europe. Would you say that these voyages tended to hasten or to delay the growth of national states? Explain.

6.3 ORGANIZE YOUR ANSWER BEFORE WRITING

You are now ready to begin answering a question. We suggest that you work first on whichever question seems easiest for you, being sure to number your answer plainly.

After rereading the question carefully to make sure you understand precisely what is being asked, add to the list of points already jotted down beside the question during the preliminary reading any additional points or details which may occur to you.

If only a one paragraph answer is expected, proceed directly to write your answer. But when longer answers are expected, you should arrange your points in a logical sequence.

Here is a suggested procedure:

1. Go through and place a check mark alongside each major idea.

2. Look over the major ideas and decide how you will order them in your essay, and write alongside each major idea the numbers 1, 2, 3, etc.

3. To support each major idea, use the remaining notes and designate them as 1a, 1b, 1c (for those points which will be used to support the first major idea), or 2a, 2b, 2c (for the points to be used in support of the second major idea), and so forth.

4. During the ordering of ideas, if you should see any gaps in either the major ideas or their supporting materials, simply insert a brief notation into the outline.

Do not spend too much time on your outline trying to make it elaborate and in exact form. An outline serves as a flexible guide, not as a rigid mold.

Reproduced below is the example from principle 6.2. The check marks, numbering system, and new points which have been added in accordance with the procedure described above are in boldface print.

2✓ *Competition bet. countries led to nationalism*
3✓ *No need for other countries for trade*
　　3a. Break Venetian Trade rts
　　3b. Italy
2b *Minerals (coffee, spices, etc.)*
2a *Wanted money + land*
1✓ *War*
2c *Cortez + Aztecs*
　　1a Unity festered from
　　2d danger within

The fifteenth- and sixteenth-century voyages of exploration produced lasting changes in the political and social structure of Western Europe. Would you say that these voyages tended to hasten or to delay the growth of national states? Explain.

When you have finished organizing the points for question one, begin writing the answer after studying the methods suggested in this chapter. When you have finished writing your answer to one question, begin to organize your answer to another. Work your way through all the questions using these suggested procedures.

6.4 WRITE TO THE POINT IF YOUR KNOW YOUR STUFF

After you have completed your brief outline, you must add muscle and skin to this skeleton. Do not, however, add any unnecessary fat. In other words, write the essentials and nothing else. Your essay should be lean and alive, not fat and slow. Your task is to be explicit, giving ample supporting material to make your outline have substance but including no irrelevant facts which may distract from your main theme.

First, in the opening paragraph write a direct answer to the question. For example, if you were given the question, "Why does Whitehead appeal to the poets for evidence concerning the nature of the objective world?", you should begin by writing "Whitehead appeals to the poets for the following four reasons...." This approach helps direct your answer to the specific question asked. Furthermore, it precludes the possibility of your shifting the answer even slightly to an area about which you may have more information.

Second, devote all subsequent paragraphs to supporting, amplifying, and modifying every point made in the first paragraph. This can be done by giving, where appropriate, dates, names, examples, and exceptions, as well as by explicitly stating relationships, causes, and effects.

Third, make your answer clear. Lead the reader neatly through the paper by well-chosen "transitional" and "directional" words. For example, if you are making an amplification, write, "to amplify ..."; if an exception, write, "the exception is ..."; if comparing, write, "on the one hand ... and on the other ..." Leave nothing to chance. Tell the instructor exactly what you are doing.

If you know your material, but write like a person who is bluffing, how is the examiner expected to know the difference? He cannot be sure. He may, if he is not too tired, notice that the paper contains facts scattered about, but could those facts have been mentioned just by chance? So, if you know your stuff, there is no better way to convey this message to the examiner than by adhering to the three suggestions stated directly above.

Following are examples of a good and a poor answer to the same question. Our comments in the left margin point out their relative strengths and weaknesses.

A GOOD ANSWER

Starts with a direct answer to the question

The exploration of the 15ᵗʰ and 16ᵗʰ centuries hastened the growth of national states. The reasons have to do with war, money and trade; and danger, wealth prestige, pride.

Preoutlines the topics and order

Starts one of the reasons

One of the prime ingredients for the beginning of national states was a common danger from the outside. Because countries went to war over the right to control certain colonies and trade routes, they had to unite, in order to within fight off an aggressor.

Transition

Other forms of competition between one country and another contributed to the growth of national states. Each country was eager Competition for land and wealth was fierce. The resources of the new lands (such as coffee, spices, minerals)

Specifics given

were considered valuable. Each country was eager to gain land because the products of the land meant more wealth, as when Cortez

Specifics given

Conquered the Aztecs. A united country could best succeed in this form of competition.

Adds a phrase to show relevance of the point to the question

These rivalries brought about by the new discoveries, increased the power of mercantilism. With the opening of new trade routes, the Northern and Western European states were able to break the Venetian-Arab trade monopoly with the Indies. The colonization led to a system involving a state-controlled market between the colony and the mother country. This

Adds an afterthought added to make sure the relation of the point to the question is clear

permitted the nations of Europe to become economically a condition which fostered nationalism. separate units, with no common market existing between them.

Amplifies with an example

It is interesting to note that Italy which did very little exploration, took longer to become a united nation than did the other countries of Europe.

Transition

Another feature in producing national states was national pride the prestige, these voyages tended to produce. The

A new point which came to mind during the writing of this answer → *voyages were financed by a national government. Any new discovery was associated with the sponsoring government and added to the spirit of nationalism.*

_____

_____

A POOR ANSWER (For ease of reading, the poor answer has been typed with mechanical errors corrected.)

Interesting, but what relevance does this have to the question?

But how does all this strengthen nationalism?

No reasons given. Only a conclusion is being stated.

Competition, wealth, trade, and pride are

The voyages of exploration is a rather ambiguous term because actually there was no sudden burst of interest in exploring the world around them—they just were looking for easier trade routes to the Orient. This so-called age of exploration if it was indeed exploring was quite by accident.

When the first countries colonized the "New World" every other country now wanted to get in on it. However, to make voyages in the first place, knowledge was needed in shipbuilding and navigation. Henry the Navigator bettered the conditions of European states by contributing to navigation, maps, etc. He also began a school for navigation. Great effort was now put forth to build more and more ships and for each country to go and colonize for itself. An example of this would be when Spain started some colonies in the "New World," France, England, Holland, etc. started sending explorers and colonizers out.

So, the voyages of exploration didn't delay the growth of the national states. The voyages were all a part of the national states. The explorers who reached other lands claimed their find for their countries. These many voyages induced the growth of the national states.

I think these voyages of exploration bound a nation together. The reason for this is that anything a group of people do to-

all suggested — but their relation to the development of nationalism is hard to see.

gether, and this was done by a whole country not just its leaders, tends to unite them. Many times newly discovered lands brought great wealth to the mother country and new places for people to settle and raise families. Then when trading was carried out with the newly found places this again helped to unite the nation. People were also united in a common cause, this being to beat other countries to these places, for trade and colonization. The lands that were claimed, and the prestige and trade that followed these voyages, affected all the people of the country and made it stronger and richer.

One practical question students frequently ask is: Should I include in my answer some facts which I know even though I am not sure they are relevant to the question? Our suggestion is that if you feel the material has a reasonable chance to be relevant, state it ever so briefly to make the instructor realize that you are familiar with it. That part of the answer should, perhaps, be footnoted to minimize its interference with the logical flow of your answer.

6.5 WRITE SOMETHING FOR EVERY ESSAY QUESTION YOU ARE ASKED TO ANSWER, EVEN IF YOU DO NOT KNOW YOUR STUFF

It is rare that the instructor will ask you a question about which you know *absolutely nothing*. Since almost all instructors give partial credit on essay questions, it is worth your time to marshal the fragments you do know into an answer, though incomplete.

Perhaps the best way to indicate how this can be done is with an illustration. Notice in the following example that the student was not familiar enough with the writings of either Coleridge or Tennyson to back up either choice with solid, detailed evidence. Although this gap precludes his receiving a perfect score (or possibly even a good score), it is unlikely that he would receive a zero—the score he would be sure to get if no answer whatever were written. Notice in the example how the student was able to make effective use of his ability to analyze his deficiency. Also, there is hardly any padding or bluffing, which more times than not irritates the grader.

> *Question* Would you say that the poetry of Coleridge or Tennyson was more in the tradition of "romanticism"? Give evidence to support your answer.
>
> *Answer* Tennyson's writings are considered to be in the Victorian tradition, whereas Coleridge is regarded as a major romantic poet. On this basis, I would answer Coleridge. A more complete answer would make liberal use of examples from each of their writings to justify this choice. Since I am not able to quote from their works, I cannot provide that kind of an answer.
>
> If I were to have samples of their writings before me, I would look to see which ones had those characteristics more nearly resembling those ascribed to romantic literature. These include the tendency toward the supernatural, the love sentiment, the extravagant incident, and the picturesque description. Perhaps its most revealing attribute is its disposition to exalt imagination, feeling, intuition, and emotional truth—often at the expense of reason and judgment. My guess is that these characteristics are found more often in the poetry of Coleridge.

6.6 ANSWER IN OUTLINE FORM IF TIME DOES NOT PERMIT A COMPLETE ESSAY ANSWER

If in spite of your good intentions you run short of time, then outline an answer in which you put down the main points of your intended composition. An answer in good outline form is far superior to an answer in fragmentary form or one that is left blank. Many teachers will grade you on the number of actual ideas or points you make rather than on the amount of verbiage that surrounds any one idea or point.

6.7 WRITE LEGIBLY

Make sure the instructor can read what you write. Above all, do not scribble. Contrary to popular belief, most graders do *not* give the student the benefit of the doubt when they cannot read what is written.

For neatness' sake we suggest double-spacing your answers, using generous side margins, and leaving extra space between answers. All these techniques will permit you to insert new material without messy cramming.

7.

SENTENCE COMPLETION ITEMS

Sentence completion items are sentences in which one or more words, symbols, or numbers are missing. The student must *recall* a suitable answer and complete the sentence. The sentence completion item lies between the short essay question in which the student must *create* or *develop* an answer and the objective test item (Chapter 8) in which the student must merely recognize the correct answer in a listing of several alternatives.[1]

An example of a sentence completion item is:

The beloved pupil of Aristotle was _____, *the son of Philip of Macedonia. (Answer: Alexander)*

[1] One of the subtests of the Scholastic Aptitude Test used to measure the ability to understand and to use the English language consists of sentences having one or more blank spaces. These particular items are not considered in the present chapters since the student's task is to recognize the best word or sets of words from several alternative answers rather than recall the correct answer. Such a multiple-choice item–type is discussed in the next chapter. Students wishing to learn more about the SAT item–type just mentioned may write to The College Entrance Examination Board, Publications Order Office, Box 592, Princeton, New Jersey 08540 and ask for a free copy of "A Description of the College Board Scholastic Aptitude Test."

In sentence completion items of the recall type, there is usually only one answer. Occasionally, however, some items lend themselves to several answers, all of which may be correct. Because definite answers are required, sentence completion items are used primarily to test for specific information. Facts must be known. For this reason, on sentence completion tests, the test-wise student has but little advantage over the student who is not so test-wise.

There are, however, some test-taking strategies which may be used when the correct answer is in doubt.

7.1 GUESS

There is never a penalty for guessing on recall-type items; therefore always write in some answer. Even an exceedingly general answer may earn partial credit. Try the following item.

_____ *wrote Don Quixote. (Answer: Cervantes)*

The answer, "a Spanish author," while grossly general and far from the correct answer of "Cervantes," is nevertheless better than no answer at all. (A flippant answer such as "someone" is, of course, worse than no answer.)

As another example, consider the following question.

Einstein published his papers in which he formulated his Special Theory of Relativity in _____.
(Answer: 1905)

If the exact date escapes you, an answer of "early in his career," although not exactly (or even grammatically) correct, may earn partial credit. The answer "the early 1900s" would be a still better attempt if you had such knowledge.

If you know from previous experience that your instructor requires exact answers without exception, then your answer, though necessarily a guess, should be in exact terms.

In instances where you cannot decide between two answers, this technique may be used: Commit yourself definitely to one, but also mention the other. Assume, for example, that you are considering both Pegasus and Poseidon as answers to the following test item.

> *According to Greek mythology, the lord and ruler of the sea is* _____. *(Answer: Poseidon)*

Assume further that you lean slightly toward Pegasus. If you must choose one, we suggest your answer be written as follows,

> *Pegasus (or possibly Poseidon).*

The obvious advantage of such an answer is that if the one you chose is wrong, at least you have shown the test maker that you not only knew but also actively considered the other, Poseidon. Better still, you might get partial credit.

7.2 MAKE THE COMPLETED STATEMENT LOGICALLY CONSISTENT

The portion of the sentence completion item which is presented places restrictions on the kinds of answers that are logically permissible. For example, the item

> *An important function of the human liver is* _____.

requires an answer which identifies some important task that the liver fulfills in the human body. Another aspect of this principle will be encountered in principle 8.3.

7.3 MAKE USE OF GRAMMAR TO HELP DECIDE THE CORRECT ANSWER

a. The word *an* immediately before the blank space indicates that the intended answer begins with a vowel. The use of *a* probably means that the intended answer begins with a consonant. Careful test makers,

however, will use this form: "*a (an)* _____."
When they do, such clues are eliminated.

b. The use of certain modifiers in the sentence may indicate the degree of generality desired in the answers. Try to answer the following test item before reading the explanation.

> *The plans for the invasion of Germany during World War II were devised by the General* _____
> _____.

Were you tempted to write in the name of some famous army general, such as Eisenhower, Marshall, or Montgomery? The presence of the word *the* before *General* rules out a name of a person because it does not fit the structure of the sentence. The intended answer is "Staff."

7.4 CONSIDER THE NUMBER AND LENGTH OF THE BLANKS TO BE FILLED IN

Some test makers use two or more separate but consecutive lines to indicate that a multiple-word response is desired. Other test makers, however, offer no such clues; they use a single line even though a two or three word response is wanted. Our point, nevertheless, is: When clues are present, use them to arrive at a correct answer.

Clues to the length of the desired response can also be discerned by the length of the blank lines. This suggestion is not too reliable, and consequently it should be used discriminatingly.

**OBJECTIVE
TEST ITEMS**[1]

Objective tests are most frequently composed of multiple-choice, true-false, and matching test items. These tests are called "objective" because the same examination paper corrected by several different people will yield the same score in each case (assuming, of course, the use of the same answer key). An essay-type test graded by several different people, however, will usually yield several different scores, some widely divergent.

Though the objective test is sometimes used to measure the recall of simple facts, in more and more cases today it is used to measure profound concepts and subtle discriminations as well as creative abilities in novel problem situations.

There are some students who do poorly on objective tests for various reasons, such as inaccurate reading of the questions, inability to detect subtleties, or just possession of the negative mental set "I never know what the test maker wants!" If you do not do well on objective tests, particularly

[1] This chapter is based on "An Analysis of Test-wiseness," by Jason Millman et al. This technical analysis appears in *Educational and Psychological Measurement*, vol. 25, no. 3, 1965. Direct quotations are not referenced.

on multiple-choice items, then this chapter and its accompanying practice set of problems will be especially helpful.

8.1 REMEMBER THE GENERAL PRINCIPLES OF TEST-TAKING

All the principles in Chapter 1 through 5 have relevance for answering objective items. Four principles which bear most directly on objective tests are recapitulated as follows:

a. *Use time wisely.* Do not spend excessive time on any one question. It is urgent that time be budgeted to permit an honest attempt at *every* question.

b. *Read directions and questions carefully.* Know what the time limits are, how to answer the questions, and how they will be scored. Be especially alert to the key terms, knowing that just one word misread or misinterpreted may lead to an incorrect answer.

c. *Attempt every question.* Remember that questions which *look* complicated and involved may not be so difficult once you get into them.

d. *Actively reason through the questions.* Some students passively stare at problems, hoping that correct answers will somehow pop up as if by magic. This is wishful thinking. Correct solutions come about when thinking about each part of the problem is aggressive and continual.

8.2 CHOOSE THE ANSWER WHICH THE TEST MAKER INTENDED

You hurt no one but yourself when you read into a question qualifications and interpretations clearly not intended by the test maker. For example,

> *Thomas Jefferson wrote the Declaration of Independence. (True or False)*

Some students might object to answering *true*, saying that four other men were also on the writing committee. The sophisticated test taker, however, would answer *true* because he would realize that this was the answer which the test maker intended for the particular level of instruction and learning which his course had reached.

Now, if the test maker had intended to find out whether you were aware that the document was written by a committee, his test item might read like this,

> *Thomas Jefferson alone wrote the Declaration of Independence. (True or False)*

In this case the answer is *false*.

In the event that you know some facts that are beyond the level of sophistication of the test, we suggest the following procedures: On teacher-made tests, record the intended answer, and then in the margin of the paper or in class, point out the possible ambiguity and make a case for a different answer. When you receive credit for the intended answer, your argument for a different answer will carry more weight because you are not arguing to persuade the teacher to change your score. On standardized tests, always choose the option which you believe has the greatest chance of being correct, even though others have merit and even though the chosen option is not completely satisfactory.

8.3 ANTICIPATE THE ANSWER, THEN LOOK FCR IT

Always anticipate what the answer will be like; then look for it among the options. This step should be accomplished very quickly. Though you may not anticipate exactly the answer that is called for, you can often anticipate some of the logical characteristics of the correct answer. For example,

> *Why is Cavalieri's Principle important in solid geometry?*

Assuming the answer is not known, you could still logically anticipate that the correct answer will clearly be a *reason* why the principle is *important*. On that basis, options which are not reasons and reasons which are not important may be eliminated, freeing you to center your attention on the remaining option or options. Let us now apply this principle of anticipation to the full problem.

> *Why is Cavalieri's Principle important in solid geometry?*
> a) *It shows that the surface area of a cube of side "s" is 6s².*
> b) *It contradicts the principles of Euclid and Gauss.*
> c) *It provides the basis for finding the volume formulae for many solids.*

The question is especially difficult if you have never heard of Cavalieri's Principle. Nevertheless, by using the principle of anticipation, you can object to option (a) because it seems too specific to have an *important* bearing on the wide field of solid geometry. Option (b) should also seem unattractive because it is negative in its "contribution" to solid geometry and because it is implausible. Option (c) possesses the anticipated ingredients of being a reason and having both a wide and an important bearing on the field of solid geometry.

8.4 CONSIDER ALL THE ALTERNATIVES

Read and consider all the options even though the first option may have all the characteristics which you anticipated. This procedure of suspended judgment is especially pertinent when dealing with multiple-choice tests of the pick-the-best-answer variety. In such tests, all the options to a question may be true, but one is the best. Because students do jump at the first plausible option, test makers frequently place their most attractive "decoy" first.

8.5 RELATE OPTIONS TO THE QUESTION

When the anticipated answer is not among the options, promptly discard it and concentrate on the given options by systematically considering how well *each* one answers the question. If you continue to hold on to your answer (which you may think is quite ingenious) or if you consider the options without continually relating them to the original question, then these pitfalls await you.

First, by not relinquishing the anticipated answer, you increase the tendency to choose an option which bears only a superficial resemblance to it. You can still be saved from this pitfall by asking yourself whether this "close cousin" is the correct answer *to this specific question.* This procedure forces you to relate options to questions.

Second, when none of the options listed appeals to you, you may be tempted to alter one or more words in an option to make it "correct." Do not *force* the answer; rather, test each real option against the real question.

Third, if you ponder the options without relating them continually to the question, you may pick an option which is *correct* in itself, but *incorrect* as it relates to the question. It is possible that *all* the listed options are correct statements, but only one of them will be the correct answer to the question. For example,

> *A spinning baseball curves because*
> *a)* The airspeeds on either side of the ball are un-equal.
> *b)* The ball is spherical.
> *c)* The momentum of the ball is equal to the product of its mass and its velocity.

Since both options (b) and (c) are true, many students would narrow their attention to these, probably choosing (c) because the words *momentum, mass,* and *velocity* pertain to a thrown baseball. Such narrowing of attention is akin to "tunnel vision." To avoid this pitfall, remember never to deal with options in isolation. (a) is the correct answer.

Finally, just as *correct* statements can be wrong answers to some questions, so can *wrong* statements be correct answers to other questions. "The world is flat" is an *incorrect* statement, but it is the correct answer to the following question: "In the 15th century most European mariners feared to sail westward on the Atlantic because they believed that. . . ." This example illustrates again the need continually to relate the options to the question. (See the two examples under principle 4.4.)

8.6 BALANCE OPTIONS AGAINST EACH OTHER

When several options look good, or even if none look good, compare them with each other. If two options are highly similar, study them to find what makes them different. For example,

> *The French Revolution of the 18th century was mainly the result of:*
> a) *American objections to the extension of slavery.*
> b) *The oppression by the Parisian middle classes of the French nobility.*
> c) *The oppression by the Bourbon monarchs of the French peasantry.*
> d) *Overproduction of food.*

Most students would probably eliminate options (a) and (d) as unlikely answers, leaving both (b) and (c) for further consideration. Options (b) and (c) are similar in that they both deal with the topic of *oppression*. But they are different in that (b) asserts that the nobility was oppressed by the people, a most unlikely situation; and (c) points out that the nobility oppressed the people, a most usual and likely situation. Option (c) is correct, of course.

8.7 USE LOGICAL REASONING

To free you to concentrate on fewer options, eliminate those which you know are incorrect, as well as those which obviously do not fit the "promise" or requirements of the question. For example,

> *The nose*
> a) *develops during gastrulation.*
> b) *has two movable joints.*
> c) *is structured in part by the turbinals.*
> d) *is an organ of balance.*

The sophisticated test taker would eliminate options (b) and (d) and choose between (a) and (c).

Logical reasoning is exemplified in a situation in which, say, you recognize that two or more options are correct, and that one of the remaining options encompasses both of these. In such a situation, always choose the more encompassing option. The following example and explanation will help to make this principle clear.

> *Which of the following cities are in the State of New York?*
> a) *Syracuse.*
> b) *Rome.*
> c) *Albany.*
> d) *All of the above.*
> e) *None of the above.*

The test-wise student who knew that two of the cities (*Syracuse* and *Albany*) were in New York State but who had never heard of *Rome*, New York, would automatically choose the encompassing answer (d) *All of the above.*

8.8 USE INFORMATION OBTAINED FROM OTHER QUESTIONS AND OPTIONS

Especially in teacher-made tests which cover a limited number of facts and concepts, one question may contain information which may be helpful in answering some other questions. For example,

The speaker in Tennyson's Maud: A Monodrama
- *a)* *marries young.*
- *b)* *goes to Germany.*
- *c)* *kills the brother of his fiancee in a duel.*
- *d)* *is a miser.*

Another question may be as follows,

Who wrote Maud: A Monodrama?
- *a)* *Hawthorne.*
- *b)* *Emerson.*
- *c)* *Thoreau.*
- *d)* *Tennyson.*

The answer to this question is obviously (d) since the information is revealed in the previous question. Although such "giveaways" are not very frequent, you should realize that you can learn as you proceed through a test, and you should be aware of the existence of information that other items on a test can provide.

For example, on standardized tests the questions are usually arranged in order of increasing difficulty. Thus, be suspicious of any question which appears much *harder* than those around it, especially near the beginning of a test, for you may be making it more difficult than it really is. Likewise, do not let down your guard when you encounter a seemingly *easy* question among the harder questions near the end of the test.

8.9 LOOK FOR SPECIFIC DETERMINERS

Some specific determiners are such words as *rarely* and *usually* which qualify the main statements in questions. Many students find these qualifying words perplexing. We cannot guarantee that you won't ever find them perplexing, but we do have some advice based on experience.

Since so many statements have exceptions, true statements often contain qualifying words and false ones often do not. But you cannot rely totally on this technique, because an experienced test maker carefully mixes up his items so that some statements with qualifiers are false and some statements without qualifiers are correct.

Another class of specific determiners is exact terms such as *always* and *none*. These words should be taken literally. When a statement is qualified by the word *always*, it means not 98 or 99 percent of the time, but a full 100 percent of the time.

A list of specific determiners is provided in Appendix I, section 3. They should be taken seriously.

8.10 MARK STATEMENTS TRUE ONLY IF THEY ARE TRUE WITHOUT EXCEPTION

Though this principle is an extension of principle 8.9, its importance deserves separate discussion.

This is the principle most often violated on true-false tests by inexperienced test takers. To eliminate this error, you must firmly believe that when you mark an answer *true*, you mean that it is *always*, 100 percent true. For example,

> *Families with more children are poorer than families with less children.*

This true-false question is *false*, because it is not *always* true that larger families are poorer than smaller families. The statement would be *true*, however, if a qualifier such as *usually*, *on the average*, or *generally* was added.

8.11 ALWAYS GUESS IF IN THE LONG RUN YOUR CHANCES OF GAINING POINTS ARE GREATER THAN YOUR CHANCES OF LOSING POINTS

Always guess on objective tests when there is no penalty for guessing. The scores on almost all teacher-made tests and many standardized tests are based on the number of correct answers only. Obviously on all such tests you have nothing to lose but rather something to gain by guessing. On tests which do have the usual correction-for-guessing factor, if you can eliminate just one option as unlikely to be correct, you will probably come out further ahead by guessing from among the others, than if you had simply skipped such questions.

The purpose of this principle is not to teach you how to get something for nothing; rather, the purpose is to spell out what must be done to earn a score which more accurately represents your full as well as partial knowledge.

Most students know some portions of a subject extremely well and other portions of the same subject not so well. Consequently, if you answer *only* the questions about which you have adequate knowledge and skip the questions on which you have partial knowledge, then your scores will not be accurate indicators of what you know.

For example, suppose on a true-false test of ten items you knew four well, but had only fragmentary knowledge about the other six items. If you answered only the four items, your highest possible score would be four out of ten. But if you had attempted all ten, your score would most likely be seven or eight correct. Which score is fairer? Don't you believe that you deserve some extra points for items about which you have partial knowledge?

8.12 DO NOT RELY ON FLAWS IN TEST CONSTRUCTION

Relying on flaws in test construction or on cues is not recommended for three reasons: First, the time spent looking for flaws could be better used in tackling the test straightforwardly; second, guessing on the basis of some extraneous cue is usually less profitable than guessing on the basis of content; and third, learning to lean on cues will be detrimental when you take the major tests of national reputation, which seldom have the types of flaws described below.

We recognize that many items of teacher-made tests contain flaws. We believe that after a test is over, students would be doing both themselves and the teacher a service to discuss with him the obvious cues. After all, future tests will probably provide not only a greater challenge, but also a greater learning experience.

On a poorly constructed test the correct option will generally, but not always show these characteristics:

a. *Length:* It will be longer than the incorrect options.

b. *Qualification:* It will be qualified to give it precision.

c. *Generalization:* It will be generalized to give it wider application than the incorrect options.

d. *Physical position:* It will *not* be the first or last option.

e. *Logical position:* It will *not* be one of the extremes of a set of options which can be put in some natural order (e.g., options which are all numbers).

f. *Similarity or oppositeness:* It will be one of two similar statements, or it will be one of two options which state the idea or fact diametrically opposite.

g. *Phraseology:* It will be in a sentence bearing familiar or stereotyped phraseology.

h. *Language:* It will *not* contain language or technical terms which you are not expected to know.

i. *Grammar:* It will be a grammatically perfect extension of the question itself.

j. *Emotive words:* It will *not* contain such extreme words as nonsense, foolhardy, harebrained, etc.

k. *Silly ideas:* It will *not* be a flippant remark or a completely unreasonable statement.

Never answer on the basis of these clues when you have any other reason to believe that one option is most likely to be correct.

PROBLEMS FOR PRACTICE

Questions

Directions Your score will be the number of questions answered correctly. Mark the *best* answer.

Although many questions will seem very difficult, you will do better than you think you are capable of doing if you apply the principles in this chapter.

1. Match the titles with the correct descriptions.
   - ( ) 1. Planting a sloping field alternately with rows of corn, then rows of wheat, then rows of corn, etc.
   - ( ) 2. Plowing a crop under instead of harvesting it.
   - ( ) 3. Removing brush and weeds along the fence between the fields.
   - ( ) 4. Planting around a hillside in level rows instead of planting up and down the hill.
   - ( ) 5. Planting a field one year with wheat, the second with oats, the third year with alfalfa, the fourth year with corn.

   Titles
   a) Clean Farming
   b) Contour Farming
   c) Crop rotation
   d) Green Manuring
   e) Strip Cropping

2. True or False (Answer each of the four parts *true* or *false*.) The word *steep*
   _____ a) is not usually used as a verb.
   _____ b) is not used as a verb.
   _____ c) is usually used as a verb.
   _____ d) is used as a verb.

3. South Dakota was admitted to the Union as the
   a) 4th state
   b) 14th state
   c) 40th state
   d) 49th state

4. Milk is considered an excellent food because
   a) milk tastes very good to many people.
   b) milk is relatively cheap considering that it is a superior food product.
   c) milk contains many vitamins and minerals.
   d) milk is used in the preparation of a variety of food products.

5. "A Shepherd's Boy (he seeks no better name)
   Led forth his flocks along the silver Thame,
   Where dancing sunbeams on the waters played,
   ...."

The above are the first three lines of Alexander Pope's pastoral poem "Summer." Which of the following is the fourth line?

    a) Where wigs were worked and fancy watches made.
    b) As never yet to love, or to be loved.
    c) He jumped a brook, and trumpets played.
    d) And verdant alders formed a quivering shade.

6. Stridulation at times facilitates
    a) coordination.   c) nutrition.
    b) dispersal.   d) reproduction.

7. Three is to triple as
    a) twelve is to dozen.   c) pair is to trousers.
    b) multiply is to many.   d) two is to double.

8. Which of the following would be most helpful for determining the volume of the solid shown at the right?

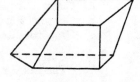

    a) Cavalieri's Principle
    b) Zeno's Paradox
    c) Simpson's Rule
    d) Wilson's Theorem
    e) Newton's Method

9. The order of mammals known as Chiroptera possesses members, commonly termed bats, which (1) have wings and fly, (2) possess a pseudocoelom, (3) will not die when infected with rabies, and (4) feed largely on gemmules. Which of the above four statements is (are) correct?

    a) only (3)   d) both (2) and (4)
    b) only (4)   e) all correct but (1)
    c) both (1) and (3)

10. True or False:
    _____ All birds fly.

11. The main advantage of using Huntington's axioms of Boolean Algebra is:

    a) If a theorem is provable from the axioms, its dual is immediately provable.
    b) Not all theorems of Brigg's Boolean Algebra can be proved from them.
    c) They are the simplest Boolean Algebra axioms to prove.

d) They are inconsistent with the properties of models of Boolean Algebras.

Answers

1. Question 1 is an example of a test item in which the associations between titles and descriptions lessen the difficulty of the question.
The associations are:

alternate rows—strip   one year wheat,
removing brush—clean   second year oats—rotation
hillside rows—contour

The answers are:

1—(e)	3—(a)	5—(c)
2—(d)	4—(b)	

Did you realize that each title could be used only once? Always check the directions or ask the test administrators for this information. Sometimes the same answer can be used more than once (see principles 8.1b and 8.5).

2. True-false questions containing either negative words such as *not* or qualifiers like *usually* require special attention. The word *steep* is used as an adjective (a *steep* hill or a *steep* price to pay) more frequently than it is as a verb (to *steep* the tea).
The answers are:

a) True   c) False
b) False   d) True

If you missed any of these questions, go back and try to reason and understand the answers given above.

3. You probably would not have known the answer to this question if the options were not given. By eliminating the least likely, you are left with option (c), the correct answer (see principle 8.7).

4. Question 4 deserves careful study because it illustrates many of the principles in this chapter. Notice that the question asks for a *reason* why milk is considered an excellent food; the correct answer, then, should be such a reason. You can logically ask yourself, "excellent food *for what purpose*?" Most likely the test maker *intended* excellent food in the sense of nutritious, good-for-you food. You should keep this in mind and choose an answer accordingly.

Options (a), (b), and (d) are all true statements, but they are not *primary* reasons why milk is an excellent (nutritious) food. For example, sugar tastes good, is relatively cheap, and is used in the preparation of many food products; yet that does not make sugar a nutritious food product. Clearly (c) is the best answer (see principles 8.2, 8.3, and 8.5).

5. Here is an unusual question which points up again the necessity of considering the possible answers in terms of the question. The fourth line must relate to the first three and be consistent with its content and rhyme scheme. *Wigs* and *watches* are not likely to be made along a riverbank where sheep graze. Options (b) and (c) have an unlikely rhyme relation to the first three lines and either represent too abrupt a change from the rural scene or contain jarring words. Option (d) is clearly the intended answer (see principle 8.5).

6. This is a difficult question. Did you guess at an answer? Remember, the directions stated that your score is the number of questions correctly answered. Since there is no penalty for guessing, you should have guessed! You should always guess when the scoring formula is "rights only" as it is in this case. The correct answer for this test item is not given since our objective was to give you practice in applying principle 8.11.

7. Did you jump at the first attractive answer, (a)? If so, reread principle 8.4. By balancing option (a) against (d) (principle 8.6), it is clear that (d), the correct answer, is superior.

8. Did you use the relevant information found in the example problem illustrating principle 8.3? If you did, you would have known that option (a) is correct. If you missed this item, review principle 8.8.

9. Here is an item in which logical thinking on your part is needed. Bats have wings and fly; thus (1) is correct. But an option with just (1) alone is not given, and the only answer which includes this statement is (c). Option (c) is the correct answer (see principle 8.7).

10. False. Statements marked true must be true *without* exception. Most birds fly, but not all. If you missed this question, review principles 8.9 and 8.10.

11. You probably do not know anything about Boolean Algebra. Even so, you can safely eliminate (b) since it is not an advantage. Because axioms are not proved, (c) is wrong. Since axioms of a system are consistent with the properties of that system, (d) is also eliminated. That leaves (a), the correct answer (see principles 8.3 and 8.5).

VERBAL ANALOGIES

Of all the various kinds of items designed to test reasoning ability, the verbal analogy items and the number and configuration series items (Chapters 10 and 11) seem to put the unsophisticated test taker at the greatest disadvantage. Such students just do not seem to get the "hang" of what is required by these test items and consequently are at a great disadvantage when competing with more experienced students. In this chapter we shall first describe the various forms of analogies, then put forth principles for solving verbal analogies.

All analogies consist of four parts (words, numbers, short phrases, or graphic elements) which bear a relationship to each other. In the analogy problem you are given two or three of the four parts, and you are asked to supply or select the missing part or parts. An example in which you are given only two of the four parts is the first of the practice problems on page 75. The following is an example in which you are asked to supply only one word of the series of four:

mother : *father* :: *wife* : _____

In this problem the first two words (*mother, father*) have a certain relationship to each other. Your task is to find a partner for the third word (*wife*) that will give the second pair the same relationship. The problem, therefore, lies in finding the relationship and applying it.

In the example above, the relationship between the first two words is one of masculine and feminine counterparts. The masculine counterpart of *wife* is *husband*. Notice that the correct answer depends on both the relationship in the first pair and the specific meaning of the third word. If the third word were *aunt* instead of *wife*, the correct answer would be *uncle*.

It is clear that analogy tests actually ask for two rather distinct types of knowledge: first, a knowledge of the words and terms used in the analogy; and second, the ability to relate these words and terms in a reasonable or logical manner. Understanding the words and terms naturally depends on your vocabulary. The following principles of test-taking can help you complete an analogy.

9.1 READ THE ANALOGY AS A SENTENCE

If the question were,

oak : tree :: Holstein : _____

you might say to yourself, "*oak* is to *tree* as *Holstein* is to what?," or "*oak* is related to *tree* in the same way as *Holstein* is related to what?" Simply saying these sentences to yourself may give you the right answer.

9.2 EXPRESS A RELATIONSHIP BETWEEN THE FIRST TWO WORDS, SUBSTITUTE THE THIRD WORD FOR THE FIRST, AND FIGURE OUT A SUITABLE SUBSTITUTE FOR THE SECOND WORD

You might express the relationship between the words *oak* and *tree* in the previous example by saying that an *oak* is a kind of *tree*. Now substitute the third word for the first in your statement (in other words, replace *oak* with *Holstein*), and see what logically follows. You would then think, "a *Holstein* is a kind of what," and you should be able to come up with the correct answer, *cow*.

If it is not immediately clear how to go from the first to the second word, try going from the second to the first. A relationship may then become clearer.

Principle 9.2 is probably the most effective and widely used procedure for solving analogy problems. Simply stated, it says to verbalize the relationship in the first pair and then apply it to the second one.

9.3 IF STUCK, EXPRESS A RELATIONSHIP BETWEEN THE FIRST AND THIRD WORDS, SUBSTITUTE THE SECOND WORD FOR THE FIRST, AND FIGURE OUT A SUITABLE SUBSTITUTE FOR THE FOURTH WORD

In some analogies for which only one part must be supplied, the most obvious relationship is between the first and third words. For example,

steel : *paper* :: *ore* : _____

The most obvious relationship is between *steel* and *ore*. That is, you can say to yourself, "*steel* is made from *ore*" and by substituting *paper* for *steel*, the correct answer becomes evident—"*paper* is made from *wood*."

9.4 BE ALERT TO COMMONLY USED RELATIONSHIPS

A high proportion of the relationships used on verbal analogy tests fall within relatively few types. The test-wise student is aware of these frequently used relationships and is on the lookout for them. A listing may be found on the next page. Each one is given as the verbal expression that you would say to yourself in solving an analogy.

Commonly Used Relationships in Verbal Analogy Tests

Relationship	Example
means the same as (opposite of)	wrath : anger
is a type of or an adjective describing	Merino : sheep
is a part of	spring : watch
usually becomes or comes before	tadpole : frog
is a cause (effect) of	puncture : "blow-out"
usually goes with	bacon : eggs
is used to (done by)	mop : clean
is used by (uses)	hammer : carpenter
is made from or made of	clothing : fabric
is a larger (smaller) version of	lake : pond
is more (less) than	hard : formidable
is a measure of	mile : distance
has the purpose of	perspiration : cooling
is located in (by or around)	Chicago : Illinois

9.5 ELIMINATE ANSWERS ON GRAMMATICAL GROUNDS

(This principle may not lead you to the correct answer, but at least you will be able to eliminate wrong answers on a multiple-choice test.) Since the completed analogy will always have pairs of identical parts of speech, you can determine what part of speech the answer should be. Consider these examples.

a) *(noun) : (noun) :: (noun) :* _____
b) *(noun) : (adjective) :: (noun) :* _____
c) *(noun) : (noun) :: (adjective) :* _____

In example (a) the missing word must be a noun; in examples (b) and (c) it must be an adjective.

PROBLEMS FOR PRACTICE

1. *gold : iron ::* _____ : _____
   a) *green : red*

    b)   maple : oak
    c)   Ford : Chevrolet
    d)   cloth : fur
    e)   full house : two pair

       This type of multiple-choice question, in which the entire second pair of words must be selected, is the item format used on the *Scholastic Aptitude Test* of the College Entrance Examination Board.

       In this particular example, the fact that both *gold* and *iron* are of the same class (metal) comes immediately to mind. All the options, however, represent pairs of words of the same class. Since more than one answer appears to be correct, it is necesary to search further for a more specific statement of the relationship between the first two words (review principle 8.6).

       Gold is much more valuable than *iron*. In the card game of poker, a *full house* is much more valuable than *two pair*. This example illustrates that analogies can be used to measure specific knowledge and vocabulary as well as reasoning ability.

       Although *cloth* and *fur* may have vastly different values, this pair is not the correct answer. The direction of the relationship is reversed. The first word of the second pair must be the more valuable of the two.

2.   *Key : card catalogue :: lock : _____*
    a) library   b) door   c) title   d) safe

       Since *key* and *card catalogue* have no obvious relationship, you should immediately try *key* and *lock*. You can say, "a *key* opens up a *lock*, so a *card catalogue* opens up a what?" *Library* is the correct response, because the *card catalogue* does provide a "key" to the contents of the *library*.

3.   *sebaceous : gastric :: skin : _____*
    a) heart b) fat c) stomach d) intestinal

       Now assume you do not know what *sebaceous* means. Can you still do the problem?

First you should notice that *sebaceous* and *gastric* are both adjectives while *skin* is a noun; the answer, therefore, must be a noun. This eliminates option (d).

You will get nothing from reciting the relationship, "*sebaceous* is to *gastric* as *skin* is to what" because we are assuming you do not know the meaning of *sebaceous*. But if you recite "*sebaceous* is to skin as *gastric* is to what" you should get a clue. You know (we shall assume) that *gastric* is an adjective describing the *stomach* so that *stomach* would be the only one of the remaining responses that could be related to *gastric*.

You can, even though you may not know one of the words in the question, use what knowledge you do have to your advantage.

4. a) 4, b) 5, c) 7, d) 6 : 12 :: 12 : 24

This numerical analogy was taken from the sample problems of the *Miller Analogies Test*.[1] The relation between the second pair can be expressed, "12 is to 24". You should then ask, "what is to 12 as 12 is to 24?" Since 12 is one-half of 24, the desired answer is 6, option (d), because 6 is one-half of 12.

You could argue that 12 is 12 less than 24 so that the right answer could be zero. That is, 12 less than 12 is zero. But this is *not* the answer, because it is not among the options.

5.

In this configural analogy (type used on a popular culture fair test of general intelligence), the relationship established by the first two boxes must be carried over into the second two boxes. One such relationship is that the second box contains both a complete and half circle, as the

[1] Reproduced by permission. Copyright © 1947, 1959, The Psychological Corporation, New York, N.Y. All rights reserved.

first one does. Thus, we can anticipate the correct option to contain both a complete and half square, as the third box does.

As we survey the six options, we find that (a), (b), (e), and (f) all contain a complete and half square. Since only one of the options can be correct, we must discriminate more sharply.

The correct option is (a) since only in this option does: (1) the small square become large, (2) the large square remain to the left of the half square, and (3) the half square rotate a half turn. That is, only option (a) has the same complex relationship to box three that box two has to box one.

10.

NUMBER
SERIES

Like the verbal analogy problem described in the preceding chapter and the configuration problem discussed in the following chapter, the solution to a number series problem involves two basic steps: (1) finding the rule and (2) applying it.

In a very real sense, both the number and the configuration series may be considered as logical extensions of the verbal analogy–type of problem. Instead of having, as in the verbal analogy problem, just one set of paired words from which the correct relationship must be ascertained, you have several numbers or several configurations to use in determining the specific relational rule.

10.1 ATTEMPT TO SPOT THE DESIRED RELATIONSHIP INTUITIVELY

Before employing the procedures for calculation discussed in the remainder of this chapter, look over a series item and see if you can quickly spot the desired relationship. If you think you see it, test it. If no relationship is immediately apparent or if the one you thought you saw doesn't test out, begin to apply the other principles in this chapter.

10.2 IDENTIFY RELATIVE VALUES OF THE NUMBERS AS THE SERIES PROGRESSES

Is every number larger in value than the preceding one? Are the numbers consistently decreasing? Do the values of the numbers both increase and decrease as the series progresses? Seek actively to find these patterns of change in numerical magnitude, for they determine the rule necessary to identify the correct relationship and solve the problem. For practice, consider the changes in direction of the values of the numbers in the six number series problems shown below.

a)	21	18	15	12	9	—				
b)	10	11	13	16	20	25	—			
c)	1	5	25	125	—					
d)	3	9	21	45	93	—				
e)	10	33	32	13	31	30	16	29	—	—
f)	2	−1	6	−4	10	−16	14	—		

In example (a) the numbers in the series are consistently decreasing, whereas in examples (b), (c), and (d) the numbers are consistently increasing. In (e) and (f) the numbers alternately increase and decrease. These six problems will be used throughout this chapter to illustrate how to apply other principles.

10.3 IF THE VALUES OF THE NUMBERS IN A SERIES FOLLOW A CONSISTENTLY INCREASING OR DECREASING PATTERN, THEN COMPUTE THE DIFFERENCES BETWEEN ADJACENT NUMBERS AND LOOK FOR A REGULAR PATTERN IN THESE DIFFERENCES

Before looking at the solution to the following number series problem, try solving it by using the above principle.

a) 21 18 15 12 9 —

Our calculations and explanations are as follows,

a)   21   18   15   12   9   —

These differences are all -3. It is now plain that the rule is: Subtract 3 from the preceding number in this series to obtain the value of the next number. In other words, the value of the last difference, which is indicated by *?*, is -3. The missing number in the series must be $9 + ? = 9 + (-3) = 6$.

Again using principle 10.3, complete the following number series.

b)   *10*   *11*   *13*   *16*   *20*   *25*   —

Our calculation and explanation are as follows,

b)   10   11   13   16   20   25   —
       1   2   3   4   5   ?

Even though this is a more difficult series, the straightforward principle of computing differences leads quickly to its solution. It is obvious that the last difference, *?*, is *6* and the missing number in the series must be $25 + ? = 25 + 6 = 31$.

Finally, try to complete the following number series using principle 10.3.

c)   *1*   *5*   *25*   *125*   —

Our calculation is as follows,

c)   1   5   25   125   —
        4   20   100

In this practice problem the differences in values between adjacent numbers do not yield an obvious pattern because the relationship is more complex. *When the differences do not provide a direct insight, then the principle discussed next should be applied.*

10.4 IF YOU CANNOT FIND AN ANSWER AFTER APPLYING PRINCIPLE 10.3, COMPUTE THE RATIO BETWEEN ADJACENT DIFFERENCES AND NOTE WHETHER THESE RATIOS ARE EQUAL

Starting from where we left off in example (c), continue trying to solve the same problem by now applying principle 10.4.

c)   1   5   25   125   —
     4   20   100   ?

The ratios of the differences are *20 ÷ 4 = 5* and *100 ÷ 20 = 5*. Note that both ratios equal 5. To find the difference, *?*, between 125 and the correct answer, solve *? ÷ 100 = 5*. That is, *? = 500*. Thus, the desired answer is 125 + *?* = 125 + *500* = 625.

For additional practice, attempt to complete the following series using principles 10.3 and 10.4.

d)   *3*   *9*   *21*   *45*   *93*   —

After using principle 10.3, the calculation should be as follows,

d)   3   9   21   45   93   —
     6   12   24   48   ?

Then, after applying principle 10.4, your calculations of the ratios of the differences should be: *12 ÷ 6 = 2; 24 ÷ 12 = 2*; and *48 ÷ 24 = 2*. If *? ÷ 48* is to equal 2 also, the value of *?* must be *96* and the correct answer must be 93 + *?* = 93 + *96* = 189.

This procedure leads to the solution of all number series problems in which there are constant relationships between adjacent numbers involving only addition, subtraction, multiplication, division, or a combination of these arithmetical operations. In example (d) above, for example, the underlying rule is: Multiply by 2 and add 3. Can you show for yourself that this rule works?

10.5 IF THE VALUES OF THE NUMBERS DO NOT FOLLOW A CONSISTENTLY INCREASING OR DECREASING PATTERN, (1) TRY TO BREAK THE SERIES INTO TWO OR MORE SEPARATE SERIES WHICH DO HAVE A CONSISTENT PATTERN AND THEN (2) FOLLOW PRINCIPLES 10.3 AND 10.4 FOR EACH SERIES

Let us begin with number series example (e).

 e) *10 33 32 13 31 30 16 29 — —*

  The procedures set forth in principle 10.5 are illustrated in the following example.

$$e) \quad 10 \overset{3}{\frown} 33 \underset{-1}{\smile} 32 \overset{}{\frown} 13 \underset{-1}{\smile} 31 \overset{3}{\frown} 30 \underset{-1}{\smile} 16 \overset{}{\frown} 29 \underset{-1}{\smile} \underline{\quad} \overset{??}{\frown} \underline{\quad}$$

Notice how the numbers in series example (e) do not follow a single consistent pattern of increasing or decreasing values. Rather, the values alternately increase and decrease, suggesting a combination of two number series, which we have separated as follows for inspection.

 33 32 31 30 29 —
    and
  10 13 16 —

The calculation of differences was probably not necessary to determine the correct missing values, 28 and 19, in this particular instance; nevertheless the practice may be helpful in future problems.

  Example (f) is presented below for practice in applying principle 10.5.

 f) *2 −1 6 −4 10 −16 14 —*

A careful perusal of the problem reveals an alternating pattern of increasing and decreasing number values, suggesting two series. A quick diagraming makes the calculation of differences easy and confirms our notion.

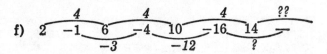

The missing number belongs to the following group within the series.

$$-1 \quad -4 \quad -16 \quad -$$

Within a group containing only 3 numbers, a wide range of defensible answers is possible for the missing number. (Incidentally, a few ambiguous test items do occur even on well-constructed tests.) You are usually on safe ground if you follow principle 10.4; that is, compute the ratio between adjacent differences. In our problem the calculation of the ratio is as follows: $-12 \div -3 = 4$. Thus if $? \div -12 = 4$, then $? = -48$, and $-16 + ? = -16 + (-48) = -64$.

10.6 IF THE PRECEDING PRINCIPLES HAVE NOT YIELDED AN AN-SWER, TRY THE FOLLOWING FIVE APPROACHES AS NEEDED—WHETHER OR NOT THE PATTERN OF NUMERICAL VALUES ALTERNATES

As an important general rule, be careful not to spend too much time on any one number series problem, especially if your testing time is highly limited.

    a. *Compare the differences with the numbers in the series.* This procedure may be helpful when the desired relationship depends on previous numbers in the series. Try to apply this rule to the following problem.

$$1 \quad 1 \quad 2 \quad 3 \quad 5 \quad 8 \quad 13 \quad - \quad -$$

The illustration and explanation of the solution follow:

$$1 \searrow \underset{0}{\nearrow} \overset{1}{\searrow} \underset{1}{\nearrow} \overset{2}{\searrow} \underset{1}{\nearrow} \overset{3}{\searrow} \underset{2}{\nearrow} \overset{5}{\searrow} \underset{3}{\nearrow} \overset{8}{\searrow} \underset{5}{\nearrow} \overset{13}{\searrow} \underset{?}{\nearrow} \overset{-}{\searrow} \underset{??}{\nearrow} \overset{-}{}$$

Except for the initial zero, the differences form the same sequence as the original series problem above. By noting the original series, we find the values of *?* and *??* are *8* and *13*. The missing numbers are $13 + ? = 13 + 8 = 21$ and $21 + ?? = 21 + 13 = 34$.

b. *Calculate differences of the differences.* This procedure may be helpful when the desired relationship changes in some regular fashion. Try to solve the following problem using this new rule.

7   17   38   81   168   —

The illustration and explanation of the solution follow,

$$7 \searrow \underset{10}{\nearrow} \overset{17}{\searrow} \underset{21}{\nearrow} \overset{38}{\searrow} \underset{43}{\nearrow} \overset{81}{\searrow} \underset{87}{\nearrow} \overset{168}{\searrow} \underset{??}{\nearrow} \overset{-}{}$$
$$\underset{11}{\searrow} \underset{22}{\nearrow} \underset{44}{\searrow} \underset{?}{\nearrow}$$

The ratios of the second differences equal 2. That is, ($22 \div 11 = 2$ and $44 \div 22 = 2$. Thus, if $? \div 44 = 2$, the value of *?* must be *88*. Since $87 + 88 = 175$, the missing value is $168 + ?? = 168 + 175 = 343$. A difficult one, we admit.

c. *Ask yourself how to get a given number from a preceding one.* Ask how you can get from the first number to the second, from the second number to the third, and so on. Or, more generally, ask what is the relationship between the first two numbers, between the next two, etc. Do not waste time trying to find simple arithmetic relationships since the procedures suggested above will identify them.

d. *Look not only for simple arithmetical rules among the numbers, but for mathematical relationships as well.* For example, the numbers may bear exponential relationships such as squares, square roots, and cubes. Try this problem.

1   3   5   7   11   13   17   19   —

These numbers are all prime numbers. Each cannot be divided evenly by any other number except itself or the number 1. The next prime number is 23. This type of problem obviously measures specific mathematical experience.

e. *Be alert for visual cues.*   Try solving this problem.

½   ⅓   —   ⅕   ⅙   ⅐

We hope that before you computed the differences, you saw that the denominators of the fractions increased by one. The missing fraction is ¼. Such problems can be solved by visual inspection.

❋

The flow diagram on page 87 may help you to see the sequence of procedures that we are recommending for solving number series problems.

PROBLEMS FOR PRACTICE

For added practice, we suggest you try to solve the following problems. Some of them, especially the last one, are quite difficult.

Questions

1.	189	93	45	21	9	—		
2.	13	8	10	16	11	13	19	—	—
3.	1	9	25	49	—			
4.	1	4	8	11	22	25	50	—	—

Flow chart of the suggested sequence of procedures
to be followed when solving number series problems

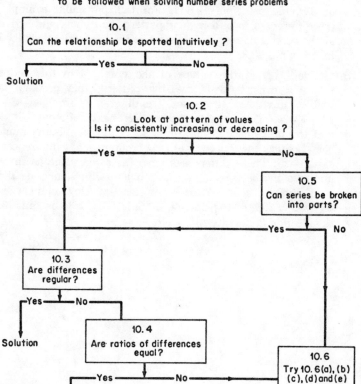

Answers

1. This is the reverse of example (d). The ratio of the differences is 2. The last difference must be *−6* and the missing number 3 (see principle 10.4).

2. If you take differences, a regular pattern of *−5, 2, 6*, will occur. Thus the missing two numbers will be 14 and 16 (see principle 10.3). You can also arrive at the correct answer by breaking the series into two groups, *13—16—19* and *8—10—11—13*, and working with differences between numbers of each grouping separately (see principle 10.5).

3. Did you recognize the series as the squares of consecutive odd numbers? The missing number is the square of 9 or 81 (see principle 10.6d). For this particular example, the differences form a regular pattern, and you could arrive at the correct answer through use of the procedure described in principle 10.3.

4. Even though the values of the numbers in this series follow a consistently increasing pattern, this problem is really a mixture of two series. The differences are *3—4—3—11—3—25*. This would suggest the next difference is *3* and the first missing number is 53. The last missing number belongs with the other grouping of differences, *4—11—25*. These differences have the same value as three numbers in the original series problem which suggests the next difference is *53* and the last missing number is $53 + 53 = 106$ (see principle 10.6a). The rule is, add 3, double, add 3, double, add 3, etc.

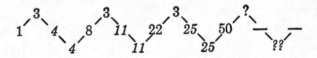

CONFIGURATION
SERIES

The configuration series problem and the number series problem are similar in that both test your ability to perceive relationships: The former uses designs; the latter uses numbers.

The configuration problem consists of a row of perhaps four designs called the "problem set," which makes a left-to-right series. From another group of designs, called the "answer set," you are to select the one design which would logically follow in the construction of the problem set.[1]

11.1 EXPRESS A RELATIONSHIP BETWEEN ADJACENT OR ALTERNATING DESIGNS AND SEE IF IT HOLDS FOR ALL DESIGNS IN THE PROBLEM SET

Consider this problem set.

[1] There is an item format that looks like a configuration *series* problem but is not. With this type of item you are to pick the design from the problem set which does *not* belong—that is, does *not* share a characteristic common to all the other designs in the set. For example, all problem set designs but one might be lacking straight edges and be constructed entirely of curved lines. Such test items (and their verbal counterparts) can have multiple "correct" answers. On tests which use this item format it is very important that you give the most plausible answer, for this will be the one intended by the test maker.

Did you notice that the number of elements in each design increases by one each time? It is often helpful to ask how does the second design differ from the first; the third from the second; and so on. (This suggestion is quite similar to principles 9.2 and 10.6c.)

Be certain that you check to see that the relationship you come up with holds true for all the designs in the problem set. Especially on configuration series problems, the unsophisticated test taker is likely to assume that a relationship decided upon after looking at *some* of the designs will hold true for *all* of them.

A reexamination of the example given above will show that the relationship suggested—the number of elements increases in each design by one—holds for the entire series.

11.2 IF NO UNIQUE ANSWER CONSISTENT WITH YOUR RELATIONSHIP RULE EXISTS, LOOK AT ALL THE WAYS THE PROBLEM DESIGNS DIFFER FROM EACH OTHER

If more than one answer or no answer seems correct, you can be certain that your first guess at the relationship rule was not specific enough, or just plain wrong. Of course, it is of the utmost importance that you do not select the first answer which seems correct without looking at all the other alternatives (review principle 8.4 in this regard).

To help clarify the ideas discussed under this principle, let us refer to the illustrative problem set given on the preceding page, but this time add an answer set.

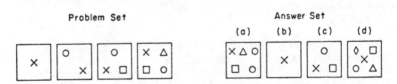

The relationship previously suggested—that the number of elements in each design increases by one—would lead us to expect an answer with five elements. Faced now with an answer set, this seemingly correct relationship no longer is satisfactory because both the (a) and (d) designs have five elements. We must either refine our rule or else come up with another one. Can you pick the correct answer? (It will be given later in the chapter.) Here are some suggestions to stimulate your thinking: What are all the ways the problem designs differ from each other? How does the second problem design differ from the first; the third from the second; the fourth from the third?

11.3 CHOOSE THE MORE PLAUSIBLE OF POSSIBLE RELATIONSHIPS

When two or more relationships are possible, each leading to a different answer design, choose the answer which the test maker most probably intended (see principle 8.2).

For example, in the configuration problem above you may have reasoned that the series was starting to repeat itself, and consequently selected a design with one element, answer (b). Or you may have reasoned that the series was starting to decrease and consequently selected a design with three elements, answer (c). Both these rules are hardly what the test maker intended since there is no concrete evidence to indicate that either a repeating (1-2-3-4-1-2-3-4) or decreasing (1-2-3-4-3-2-1) cycle was desired. Furthermore, even if you persisted in holding to these two relationships, you would not have a defensible basis for choosing one in preference to the other.

Obviously, you have to come up with another possible relationship. In this particular problem set, the relationship intended is that the next design should have not only *all* the shapes in the preceding design, but also one additional unique element as well; consequently (d) is the correct answer.

Sometimes it is difficult for the mind not only to relinquish relationships which do not fit, but also to seek other relationships from another point of view. When this happens, you are in a "rut," or in psychological terms have a strong "mental set."

To break out of a rut, we suggest that you go on to other problems. After completing them, come back to the perplexing one, for now the chances are better that you will approach it with a different mental set. One reason for coming back is that configuration problems are graded in difficulty; that is, the easier problems usually come first.

11.4 BE ALERT TO COMMONLY USED RELATIONSHIPS

This suggestion is similar to principle 9.4. Many configuration series use relatively few types of relationships. The testwise student knows them and looks out for them.

Listed below are general descriptions of design changes frequently used on configuration series tests. We suggest that you get firsthand experience in handling these common types by working the Problems for Practice at the end of this chapter. Frequently two or more of these relationships are used within the same series; consequently, the correct rule can be a combination of two simple rules joined by the word *and*.

Common Changes in Designs
Used in Configuration Series Tests[1]

1. *Relative Position.* The relationship of one or more elements of the design to the rest changes in position from one design to the next. Changes can be in a clockwise rotation, left to right, down to up, and so forth.

2. *Number.* The number of one or more parts of the design can be constant or change in some regular pattern from design to design. Changes can be in the number of elements, number of sides on a figure, and so forth.

3. *Part-Whole.* The degree of completeness of the design changes from one problem box to the next as some part of the design is deleted or some new part added. This design change can be considered a combination of 1 and 2.

4. *Changes in Scale and Shading.* The shape of the design remains essentially the same, but the elements change in actual size or in type of shading.

5. *Alternation.* Some aspect of the design is repeated in every other problem box, while another design or an aspect of the same design is repeated in the remaining alternate problem boxes.

[1] Two or more of these changes are often used together.

PROBLEMS FOR PRACTICE

Questions

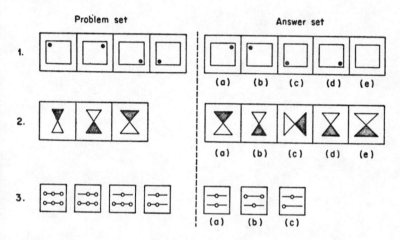

Answers

1. This question, which is used as a practice example on the *Differential Aptitude Test,*[1] illustrates a change of *relative position.* The dot moves around the square clockwise: upper-left corner, upper-right corner, lower-right corner, lower-left corner. The correct answer is (b).

2. Several changes are going on at once. The top part of the figure *alternates* black-white-black while the bottom alternates white-black-white. Not only does the shading change but the "fatness" of the figure steadily increases.

[1] Reproduced by permission. Copyright © 1947, 1961, The Psychological Corporation, New York, N.Y. All rights reserved.

Only answer (e) preserves this change in fatness and the alternation of shading.

3. One circle is being removed in each successive problem box; consequently, the answer box should logically have only two circles in it. Of the two having just two circles, box (a) and box (c), the correct one is (a) since there is no evidence to lead you to anticipate that the middle circle in the bottom row would be removed when it was not removed in the top row. In other words, only corner circles are being removed.

PART 4

**PRINCIPLES OF
TAKING TESTS
MEASURING
SELECTED
ABILITIES**

Part III contains principles and suggestions for answering questions in the forms of essay, sentence completion, objective item, verbal analogy, number series, and configuration series.

Theoretically any one of these question forms could be used to measure abilities in a great many fields. For example, essay questions could be used to test your aptitude in Art; objective questions to test your knowledge of Zoology.

In dealing thus far with question forms rather than with subject matter areas, we have provided principles and suggestions which may be generalized to all achievement and ability areas as long as the questions are in any of the above six forms. In the following four chapters our emphasis will now be on four types of *abilities* which may be generalized: vocabulary ability, reading comprehension, numerical problem-solving ability, and ability to understand graphical data.

These four abilities have been selected for two reasons: First, they are measured frequently in important examinations. Second, the basic ideas essential for doing well on tests of these abilities can be stated in principles which sophisticated test takers easily employ.

12.

TESTS OF VOCABULARY ABILITY

Standardized tests of general ability as well as tests of scholastic aptitude almost always contain vocabulary test items, perhaps because vocabulary ability is the best single indicator of general intelligence. A further, more functional use of a large and precise vocabulary is to understand the words in questions designed to measure other abilities (refer, for example, to practice problem 3, Chapter 9).

For the above reasons as well as for improving your writing and speaking ability, we urge you to use the following principles as ways for improving your overall vocabulary.

12.1 LEARN THE COMMON COMBINING FORMS, PREFIXES, ROOTS, AND SUFFIXES

Linguists have estimated that 60 percent of English words in relatively common use today are of Latin and Greek origin.

In the present as in the past, whenever new substances, processes, or ideas are found or formulated, new words to designate them are not coined arbitrarily but are usually constructed in an orderly fashion from already existing word-elements (generally Latin or Greek). For example, the word *micropaleontologist* is made up of five separate word building blocks, each of which has a meaning of its own, illustrated below.

micro-	small	*micropaleontologist* means
paleo-	old, ancient	one who specializes in
onto-	being, existing	the science of old, small
logia-	science of	forms of life (i.e., being).
ist-	one who	

Whenever you encounter a difficult word such as *micropaleontologist*, you should use the technique of divide and conquer. You know that most words are made up of logical parts, so you should try to identify some individual part or parts of a word to gain a clue which can be used in conjunction with the context of the sentence or phrase in which the word is embedded or the option words presented to arrive at an answer. Though certain of the five parts of *micropaleontologist* are more important than others, nevertheless understanding the meaning of any one part could furnish the clue to the correct answer.

Since students deal with a vocabulary which is for the most part made up of relatively few Latin and Greek prefixes and roots, we have provided two special lists on the following pages: one containing the most commonly used prefixes; the other containing the most commonly used roots and combining forms. In using these word parts, you should bear in mind that prefixes (and suffixes) are abstract, and have merely a formative function. Combining forms have coordinating functions, as in *tele*graph. Carefully learning these lists will place you on a par with most test-wise students. To aid in remembering word parts, we suggest that you establish associations by learning the definitions of actual words which contain these word parts. For example, if you learn that the definition of a *microscope* is an optical instrument used to see "small" things, then it will be easier to remember by association that *micro* means "small."

COMMON PREFIXES

Prefix	Meaning	Example	Definition
a-	not, without	atypical	not typical
an-	not, without	anarchy	without law
ab-	away from	abnormal	away from the average
ad-	to, toward	adhere	to stick to
ambi-	both	ambidextrous	using both hands equally
amphi-	around	amphitheater	auditorium with seats around a stage
ante-	before	antebellum	before the war
anti-	against, opposite	antiaircraft	defense against aircraft
ant-	against, opposite	antacid	counteracting acidity
con-	together with	confide	to trust
de-	away from	deduct	to take away from
dia-	across, through	diameter	straight line across the center of an object
dis-	apart, opposite of	disassemble	to take apart
ec-	out of	eccentric	out of center
ex-	out of	expel	to drive out of
epi-	over	epidermis	outer skin
epi-	upon	epigram	a witticism upon a particular subject
hyper-	over, beyond	hypertension	high blood pressure
hypo-	less, under	hypodermic	under the skin
in-	in, into	incorporate	to unite
in-	not	inconsistent	not consistent
inter-	between	interglacial	between glacial epochs
mis-	wrong	misconstrue	to construe wrongly
mono-	one	monolith	a single block of stone
mono-	alone	monophobia	a dread of being alone
non-	not	nonstandard	not standard
ob-	against	obstacle	a hindrance
per-	through	permeate	to spread through
pre-	before	predict	to tell beforehand
pro-	forth	progress	movement forward
pro-	before	prologue	spoken before
re-	back, again	regress	to go back
sub-	under	submarine	being under water
trans-	across	transcontinental	extending across a continent
trans-	beyond	transgress	to go beyond limits set
un-	not	unaware	not aware

COMMON ROOTS AND COMBINING FORMS

Root or Combining Form	Meaning	Example	Definition
anthrop-	man	anthropoid	resembling man
aqua-	water	aqueous	watery
arch-	chief	archrival	chief rival
aud(i)-	hear	auditor	a hearer
bio-	life	biography	the written history of a man's life
biblio-	book	bibliophile	a lover of books
cap-	take	capacious	takes in much space
-cept	take	precept	a rule for action or conduct
-ceive	take	receive	to take thing offered
cip-	take	anticipate	to take up ahead of time
chron-	time	chronic	continuing a long time
corp(us)-	body	corpulent	bulky; very fat
cred-	believe	credulous	inclined to believe
duc-, duct-	lead	induce	to lead on
fac-	do, make	facile	easily done
fact-	do, make	manufacture	to make wares
feas-	do, make	feasible	capable of being done
fect-	do, make	effective	producing desired effect
-fer	bear, carry	transfer	to carry from one place to another
-graph	write	monograph	a written account of a single thing
homo-	same	homogenous	of the same kind
-logy	science of	pomology	the science of fruit growing
mit-	send	transmit	to send to another place
mis-	send	missile	a hurled object
ped-, pod-	foot	pedestrian	one who journeys on foot
plic-	fold or twist together, to involve	implicit	involve in nature of something not revealed
plicat-		implicate	to bring into incriminating connection
pli-		pliant	easily folded or twisted
-ply		imply	to involve by indirection
psych-	mind	psychosomatic	the interrelation of mind and body
scrib-	write	describe	to give account of
-script	write	subscription	a consent by underwriting the name
sist-	stand	insist	to take a stand
spec-	look	spectator	one who looks on

COMMON ROOTS AND COMBINING FORMS

Root or Combining Form	Meaning	Example	Definition
spic-	look	conspicuous	obvious to the eye
-spect	look	circumspect	attentive to all aspects
ten-	hold	tenet	a principle held as true
-tain	hold	maintain	to hold possession of
vert-	turn	revert	to turn back
vers-	turn	reverse	to turn upside down

In addition to these lists, we have included in Appendixes II, III, and IV several longer lists of specially selected prefixes, roots, and suffixes. These lists may be used in the following three ways: first, to gain some degree of familiarity with a large number of word parts; second, to master the meanings of those word parts which you think are important; and third, to serve as a reference for the meanings of prefixes, roots, and suffixes in words you may encounter in reading or listening.

12.2 WHEN YOU ENCOUNTER UNFAMILIAR WORDS, LOOK FOR PARTS ALSO OCCURRING IN FAMILIAR WORDS

This principle is demonstrated in the following example.

> *The word* terricolosis *means*
> a) *having a respiratory disease*
> b) *seeing in the future*
> c) *riding on horseback*
> d) *living on the ground*

Terricolosis is a relatively unfamiliar word, but it does contain a part, *terri-*, which is also found in some common words familiar to most students, for example, *terrain, terrace, territory*. Since all these words are associated with land, the sophisticated test taker would find option (d) attractive, which is the correct answer in this case.

A word of caution: Answering with such partial information can backfire when the familiar word part is purposely used to direct you to an incorrect option. For example,

A talisman *is a*
  a) *bringer of luck*
  b) *seller of articles*
  c) *teller of stories*

Though it may make some sense to chose option (c), meaning a teller of *tales;* or option (b), meaning a *salesman;* nevertheless the correct option is (a).

The intent of principle 12.2 is to provide you with a technique for employing the facts you *do* know and your intelligence, rather than relying on blind chance.

12.3 IF YOU CANNOT SOLVE A MULTIPLE-CHOICE VOCABULARY ITEM, TRY THESE APPROACHES

Even though these approaches may not always be successful, nevertheless a thinking approach is better than a pure guess. If time is important, we advise your giving these approaches only a brief try and then going on.

  a. *Determine the part of speech of a word from its suffix.* By using the suffix of a word to determine whether it is a noun, adjective, or verb, you can sometimes eliminate incorrect options in multiple-choice vocabulary items.

  The brief list of suffixes which follows shows the association between specific suffixes and the parts of speech of the words which contain them.

Suffix	Part of Speech	Usual Meaning	Example	Meaning
-ot	noun	one who	patriot	one who loves his country
-ee	noun	one who receives	payee	one who receives payment

Suffix	Part of Speech	Usual Meaning	Example	Meaning
-dom	abstract noun	quality of	wisdom	quality of being wise
-ment	abstract noun	process of	government	process of being ruled
-ac	adjective	pertaining to	cardiac	pertaining to the heart
-ose	adjective	full of	verbose	full of words
-ate	verb	to make	fabricate	to construct
-esce	verb	to do	effervesce	to bubble

Several additional lists of suffixes have been included in Appendix IV.

b. *Eliminate options which are based on words that look or sound like the word to be defined.* Test makers often include incorrect options which perfectly fit a word that looks or sounds like the word to be defined. For example,

suborn *means*
   a)   *to obtain by private or unlawful means*
   b)   *to be unyielding*
   c)   *to have kindness*
   d)   *to live in wealth*

Option (b) should be eliminated from further consideration immediately because it is obvious that option (b) was constructed to trap anyone who confused or associated the word, *stubborn,* with the word, *suborn.* The correct answer is option (a).

c. *If the word to be defined is somewhat familiar, use it in a sentence and then substitute each option.* This technique was used successfully on the following vocabulary question.

adventitious *means*
   a)   *fraudulent*   c)   *evil*
   b)   *fortunate*   d)   *accidental*

A student remembered from his general science course that there were trees which grew in swamps having *adventitious* roots, but he never found out what the word meant. He constructed the sentence, "The tree has *adventitious* roots," and then tried "... *fraudulent* roots," "... *fortunate* roots," and "... *evil* roots." Though he did not know that *adventitious* meant *accidental*, he nevertheless chose this option because it fitted the constructed sentence and sounded best. He was correct.

d. *If you know a meaning of the word to be defined, but it is not one of the options, consider other meanings.* Attempt this question.

shoot *means*
  a) silent   c) new growth
  b) sleepy   d) briefly seen

It is natural to define *shoot* as "to fire a gun," but no similar definition is included among the options. When this happens, consider another meaning for *shoot*. If you think of a bamboo or asparagus *shoot*, then option (c), new growth, will make sense.

In actual practice this principle is intended to encourage you, when necessary, to think of all the related definitions of a word.

12.4 LOOK AT THE WORD IN CONTEXT

A clue to the meaning of an unfamiliar word may be seen in the context of the sentence or paragraph in which it appears.

This principle is not useful for solving the synonym-type vocabulary items used so far in this chapter. It is, however, highly useful for discovering the meanings of difficult words found in questions designed to test other abilities, or in paragraphs followed by various types of questions used to test reading comprehension.

To understand the practicality of this principle, try to answer the following synonym-type vocabulary item.

mollify *means to*
a) persuade
b) change
c) retain
d) soften
e) invalidate

Now, notice how much easier it is to ascertain the meaning of *mollify* when it can be seen in the content of this sentence taken from Washington Irving's *The Alhambra*.

> *The Alcalde was just risen. Pedrillo Pedrugo (the barber) seated him in a chair, threw a napkin round his neck, put a basin of hot water under his chin, and began to mollify his beard with his fingers.*

The standard definition of *mollify* is: "to soften; to make tender or supple; to reduce the hardness."

Practice problem 3 in Chapter 9 provides a different illustration of how the context of a test item can furnish a clue to the meaning of an unknown word.

12.5 BALANCE OPTIONS AGAINST EACH OTHER

Though this principle is identical to principle 8.6, it is sufficiently important to be repeated—this time for vocabulary tests. Many vocabulary tests try to do more than determine how many obscure words you may know. They try to measure your perceptiveness, that is, your ability to make fine discriminations among words.

Consider this vocabulary test item.

> *When making the reservation, the receptionist accidentally forgot the last "e" in Mrs. Greene's name. This _____ had little consequence.*
> a) blunder
> b) decision
> c) fault
> d) mistake

In a way, all the options have a certain appeal. By attending to their differences and more exact meanings, you will be better able to choose the correct answer.

Blunder implies gross stupidity or ignorance; *decision* conveys that a conscious choice was made; *fault* refers to an imperfection or blameworthy defect; and *mistake* expresses a misconception or misunderstanding like the one in this sample. Option (d) is correct.

Notice also the need to make fine discriminations among words in the following verbal analogy, which, in a real sense, is also a vocabulary test item.

> *heat* : *lukewarm* :: *water* : _____
> | | |
> |---|---|
> | a) *temperature* | c) *fall* |
> | b) *damp* | d) *wet* |

Options (b) and (d) are the most attractive because both convey the correct idea generally. Since both cannot be right, we must look for a discriminating relationship. Because a smaller amount of *heat* is required to make an object *lukewarm* than to make it hot, it is reasonable that a smaller amount of *water* will make an object *damp* rather than wet. Therefore, option (b) is correct.

13.

TESTS OF READING COMPREHENSION

College work demands that students be able to read with understanding, discrimination, and insight in *all* their subjects. It is probably because of the importance of these skills that nearly half the testing time on the verbal sections of the *Scholastic Aptitude Test* is devoted to questions of reading comprehension.

Comprehension questions are multiple-choice and based on different passages (often a single paragraph, sometimes a full selection) of reading material. The types of reading material may vary from technical or textbook passages to excerpts from short stories and novels.

Though there are time limits on the overall sections, there are usually no shorter internal time limits for any of the individual reading passages. Since the score depends upon how many questions are answered correctly, students use several widely varying test-taking strategies. Some read very quickly to cover as many passages and questions as possible. Others read very slowly to make sure that every question attempted is answered correctly.

The strategy we propose for taking examinations of reading comprehension is incorporated in the principles which follow.

13.1 DO NOT EXPECT TO BE ABLE TO FIND THE ANSWER TO AN INFERENTIAL QUESTION LOCALIZED WITHIN THE READING PASSAGE

There are two broad categories of reading comprehension test questions: the *explicit* and the *inferential.* Some questions call for answers which may be explicitly stated in one particular (local) portion of the reading selection. These are *explicit* questions.

Other test questions are concerned with inferences, relationships, evaluations, and the tone and intent of the author. Such questions are *inferential;* that is, they require you to choose an answer which goes beyond any single explicitly stated point in a particular portion of a reading passage. The fourth question of the first practice problem (Plato's *Republic*) at the end of this chapter is a good example of an inferential question.

The fact that reading comprehension tests contain inferential questions in increasing proportion on examinations for older students has an important implication for test taking. A student can not expect simply to skim a passage and have the answer stand out. The answer must be inferred from what he reads. Understanding the content of a passage is necessary to deal effectively with inferential questions; principle 13.2 is offered for this reason.

13.2 STRESS COMPREHENSION OVER SPEED

We believe that a slow, careful first reading of test passages will actually result in higher test scores than will an initial skimming of the material. The student who does not have a good grasp of the meaning of the passage will either miss *inferential* questions or spend an unprofitable amount of time rereading the passage. For *explicit* questions, the student who has read for comprehension will have a good idea which portion of the passage contains necessary information and will be able to locate it efficiently. Thus a careful initial reading will not only lead to a higher proportion of correct answers, but may also save time.

Slowness alone does not ensure comprehension. You must also *be aware of what you are reading.* Avoid the widespread habit of reading words instead of ideas by continually asking yourself: What is he (the author) saying? What was the meaning of what I just read? Questions like these serve as mental catalysts, transforming words into ideas.

Our suggestion to stress comprehension does not mean that you should be unconcerned with the pace at which you read; on timed tests you can never be as meticulously slow as you wish.

13.3 RETURN TO THE PASSAGE WHEN NECESSARY TO ANSWER A QUESTION

Almost all tests of reading comprehension permit you to reread the passage; therefore, if you do not know the answer to a question or are not reasonably certain of an answer, do not waste time puzzling. Go back to the appropriate portion of the passage to ferret out the answer.

It is usually a waste of time to reread the entire passage. Extract from the selection only what you need to answer the questions.

13.4 AVOID SELECTING A PARTICULAR ANSWER WHEN A GENERAL ONE IS DESIRED

As implied in principle 13.1, most questions demand answers which must be the generalized sum or essence inferred from several phrases and sentences within the total selection. *Incorrect* options for these inferential questions are often specific instances or examples, which are correct as they stand, but which do not represent the degree of generality required by the question. Look for the option which is inclusive rather than exclusive. This principle is similar to principle 8.7.

We urge that you apply the four principles outlined in this chapter to the practice exercises which follow. These principles will work for you only to the extent that you can apply them. You will also become familiar with some of the concepts on which many of the comprehension questions are based. Some important aspects of these principles are: knowing the meaning of words in context, comprehending the sense meaning of explicit statements, seeing the meaning and purpose of allusions and figures of speech, identifying patterns of development, distinguishing between emotive and nonemotive words, perceiving the author's tone, inferring the moral and philosophical implications of statements, ascertaining the purpose of descriptive elements, and sensing the author's intent.

To gain the maximum knowledge from these exercises, study especially the explanations which follow the correct answers so that you will fully understand why the correct answers are in fact correct.

PROBLEMS FOR PRACTICE[1]

Directions Each passage in this group is followed by questions based on its content. After reading a passage, choose the best answer to each question. Answer all questions following a passage on the basis of what is *stated* or *implied* in that passage.

Sample Passage (Set 1)

That Plato's *Republic* should have been admired, on its political side, by decent people, is perhaps the most astonishing example of literary snobbery in all history. Let us consider a few points in this totalitarian tract. The main

[1] The following seven sample questions are reprinted with permission from the 1968 edition of *A Description of the College Board Scholastic Aptitude Test,* published by the College Entrance Examination Board, New York. This booklet, which contains many illustrative examples of the different kinds of questions that are used in the Scholastic Aptitude Test, is revised annually and is supplied without cost to high schools for distribution to students before they take the test. The booklet may also be obtained on request by writing to College Entrance Examination Board, Publications Order Office, Box 592, Princeton, New Jersey.

purpose of education is to produce courage in battle. To this end, there is to be a rigid censorship of the stories told by mothers and nurses to young children; there is to be no reading of Homer because that degraded versifier makes heroes lament and gods laugh; the drama is to be forbidden because it contains villains and women; music is to be only of certain kinds, which, in modern terms, would be "Rule Britannia" and "The British Grenadiers." The government is to be in the hands of a small oligarchy, who are to practice trickery and lying—trickery in manipulating the drawing of lots for eugenic purposes, and elaborate lying to persuade the population that there are biological differences between the upper and lower classes. Whether people are happy in this community does not matter, we are told, for excellence resides in the whole, not in the parts.

This system derives its persuasive force from the marriage of aristocratic prejudice and "divine philosophy"; without the latter, its repulsiveness would be obvious. The fine talk about the good and the unchanging makes it possible to lull the reader into acquiescence in the doctrine that the good shall rule, and that their purpose should be to preserve the status quo. To every man of strong political convictions—and the Greeks had amazingly vehement political passions—it is obvious that "the good" are those of his own party, and that, if they could establish the constitution they desire, no further change would be necessary.

So Plato taught, but by concealing his thought in metaphysical mists he gave it an impersonal and disinterested appearance which deceived the world for ages. The ideal of static perfection, which Plato derived from Parmenides and embodied in his theory of ideas, is one which is now generally recognized as inapplicable to human affairs. Man is a restless animal. Man needs, for his happiness, not only the enjoyment of this or that, but hope and enterprise and change. As Hobbes says, "felicity consisteth in prospering, not in having prospered."

uestions and Explanations (Set 1)

1. According to the passage, Plato expresses the belief that
   a) drama may not be permitted if it omits villains and women.

b) those parts of Homer dealing with heroes and gods may be read.
c) only stories about military life may be read by the people.
d) with few exceptions, music may be enjoyed by all citizens.
e) the stories told to children should be strongly censored.

This is a relatively easy question based on a statement made in the first paragraph of the passage. The correct answer is (e). Each of the other choices is either contradicted by the passage or is a misinterpretation of the information given.

2. According to the passage, Plato's theory of ideas included
a) the ideal of static perfection.
b) an exact quotation from Parmenides.
c) the assertion that man is a restless animal.
d) the belief that man needs hope, enterprise, and change.
e) an emphasis upon individual happiness.

Question 2 is slightly below average in difficulty; it requires you to identify one of the supporting ideas in the passage. Both choices (c) and (d) represent the statements of the author regarding the nature of man, but do not represent Plato's theory. (e) refers to a quotation from Hobbes that the author uses to support his own (as opposed to Plato's) theories. The third paragraph of the passage states that Plato *derived* the ideal of static perfection from Parmenides, but does not suggest that he borrowed Parmenides' idea in its entirety. The correct answer, (a), is explicitly stated in the last paragraph of the passage.

3. The author implies that the doctrine that "the good shall rule" has been favorably received largely because
a) people assume that "the good" will eventually rule.
b) this is a doctrine that closely resembles those of divine scripture.
c) readers of the *Republic* have automatically identified themselves with "the good."
d) many people have strong political convictions.

This question of approximately average difficulty asks you to analyze one of the major supporting points made by the author and to examine closely the logic utilized. In the last sentence of the second paragraph, the author makes the point that "... it is obvious that 'the good' are those of his own party ...," and the implication here is that readers of the *Republic* have automatically identified themselves with "the good" (c).

4. The author of this passage considers Plato's *Republic* to be a work written principally for the purpose of
   a) providing citizens with a guide to the best possible life.
   b) changing existing methods of education.
   c) convincing readers that the rule of the few is preferable to the rule of the many.
   d) convincing the populace of biological differences among classes.
   e) encouraging people to overthrow existing governments.

This relatively difficult question asks you to extract from the passage and its implications the author's idea of the purpose or purposes for which Plato's *Republic* was written. The correct answer is (c). No reference is made to (e) in the passage, and although (b) and (d) are among Plato's specific means for bringing about the government that he considers ideal, they do not represent the author's view of why the *Republic* was written. (a) may have been Plato's reason for writing the work, but it certainly does not constitute the author's idea of why Plato wrote the work.

Sample Passage (Set 2)

As long ago as 1670, Montanari noted that the second-magnitude star, Algol, was sometimes fainter than usual. Goodricke, in 1782, discovered that these variations were *periodic* and occurred at regular intervals of $2^d20^h49^m$. For about 2^d11^h the star remains of substantially constant brightness. During the next five hours it loses two-thirds of its light and returns to its original brightness in the five hours following. Goodricke realized that this variation in brightness might be caused by the partial eclipse of the star by a large body revolving round it, but no other binary stars were known at that time, and his explanation was almost forgotten until revived by Pickering a century later. Thousands of stars are now definitely known to vary in this fashion.

Like their prototype, Algol, these stars usually remain at a nearly constant magnitude for some time, following which their brightness decreases rapidly to a minimum. The light may remain constant at the minimum for some time or only for a moment, but in either case the increase to normal is as rapid as the decrease. After remaining practically stationary for some time the brightness falls again, usually much less than before and sometimes almost imperceptibly, then rises again to normal and remains stationary for about the same time as before, after which the whole cycle is repeated with very exact periodicity. The deeper minimum is called the *primary minimum*, the other, the *secondary*.

The difference in brightness between the variable star and a neighboring comparison star of constant brightness is repeatedly measured with a photometer and the time of each observation noted.

This characteristic change in brightness is readily explained on the assumption that the variable star is a binary pair with components usually differing in size and brightness, and that the orbital plane is nearly edgewise to the line of sight from the earth, so that the components eclipse one another during every revolution. When the fainter star begins to pass in front of the brighter, the light from the system begins to decrease.

Questions and Explanations (Set 2)

1. The time for Algol's passage from its maximum brightness through its primary minimum and back again is approximately
   a) 1.5 min.
   b) 16 min.
   c) 1.5 hr.
   d) 10 hr.
   e) 20 hr.

This is a "plain-sense" question, involving the first paragraph of the passage and requiring very simple computation. If Algol loses two-thirds of its light during five hours (as stated in the fourth sentence) and requires another five hours to return to its original brightness, then the total time is obviously ten hours, answer (d). You can also compute the correct answer by subtracting 2^d11^h from $2^d20^h49^m$, which gives roughly ten hours.

If you understood the terms "maximum brightness" and "primary minimum," which are explained in the second paragraph, you should have no difficulty with this next question.

2. The primary minimum occurs when the
   a) fainter star passes in front of the brighter star.
   b) plane of the orbit changes.
   c) two stars are side by side.
   d) fainter star is moving away from the earth.
   e) binary pair is moving away from the earth.

If you read the second paragraph carefully, you should understand that the primary minimum is the period of lesser brightness. The fourth paragraph in the passage states that the decrease in brightness is caused by the eclipse of the brighter star by the fainter star in the pair. The correct answer, therefore, must be (a).

(This question does not require that you understand the difference between the primary and secondary minima, since this distinction is not called for by any of the possible choices. However, by careful reading of the passage you can infer that the secondary minimum is an eclipse of the fainter by the brighter of the pair of stars.)

3. Which of the following offers the most reasonable explanation of why a neighboring comparison star of constant brightness is used in making variable star observations?
   a) Two measurements are always more accurate than one.
   b) The neighboring star's variations can be plotted at the same time.
   c) Two stars which appear close together in the sky are usually of about equal brightness.
   d) It is necessary to adjust for atmospheric factors affecting visibility.
   e) Stars in the same part of the sky are all about equally distant from the earth.

This question is much more difficult than the two preceding it. In order to answer it correctly, you must examine logically the possible reasons for using the photometer to which reference is made in the third paragraph of the passage. The correct answer, (d), is the only one that provides an insight into the difficulties usually encountered by an astronomer when he makes observations, that is, the effects of fluctuations of the earth's atmosphere upon precise observation. Of course this question requires more than just a brief examination of the passage, but the logical reasoning processes involved are those that the critical reader will use.

Although all the incorrect choices appear to be reasonable statements, they constitute insufficient and illogical reasons for the procedure described in the passage.

14.

**TESTS OF
NUMERICAL
PROBLEM
SOLVING ABILITY[1]**

Solutions for problems involving numbers or symbols may be broken down into four steps: understand the problem, find a way to use what is known to solve for what is unknown, carry out this procedure, and check the work. Each of these steps will be considered in turn.

14.1 UNDERSTAND THE QUESTION OR PROBLEM BEING ASKED

Before starting on the problem, be sure you clearly understand what you are supposed to find, what is required to find it, and what is the unknown. Pay particular attention to key terms (e.g., isosceles, rate, tangent), and consider whether drawing a sketch will help you to comprehend what is being asked. Do you know the form in which the answer should be? Are you expected to calculate a numerical answer? Is an algebraic expression of the value of one quantity in terms of others desired? Is a proof required?

[1] This general approach is recognized by G. Polya in his book *How to Solve It: A New Aspect of Mathematical Method*, 2d ed., Doubleday & Company, Inc., Garden City, N.Y., 1957.

14.2 FIND A METHOD TO SOLVE FOR WHAT IS UNKNOWN

There is a tremendous variety of problems which require the use of numbers or symbols. It is, of course, impossible to state one procedure which will be successful for solving all these types. The following group of questions, however, will frequently help you to find a way to use what is known to solve for what is unknown.

1. Have you kept in mind what you are trying to find or prove?

2. Have you written down *all* that is given or known? Are there things that you know from the definition of terms? For example, in a problem about an equilateral triangle have you written down that the three sides are equal?

3. Have you drawn a good sketch when appropriate? An accurate drawing may show certain relations which could help solve an intermediate problem. Have you labeled all that you know and all the unknowns? Have you recorded other facts which are easily known, or can be proved, from the given data? Did you erroneously draw a special case when the problem is more general? For example, did you draw a right triangle when the problem does not specify the type of triangle?

4. Are you using good notation? Does each symbol stand for only one thing or equal things? Is the notation consistent with the symbolism used in the formulas with which you are accustomed?

5. Have you written down relevant formulas containing any or all the given symbols?

Even after you have considered all the questions above, the procedure for solving the problem may still escape you. Here are some things you can consider when you get stuck.

1. Have you used *all* the data and other facts presented in the problem?

2. What can you find with the data? Are there some

things you can prove or quantities for which you can solve? If so, perhaps this can be helpful and serve as an intermediate step.

3. Look at what you have to find. Can you recall other problems which have had such an unknown? If so, how did you solve them? (The value of practice problems is evident here.)

·4. Consider using certain theorems or formulas that seem to be related to the material in the problem.

5. Try working backward. To solve the problem, what information do you need? How can you find what you need to know? Continue working backward.

6. Consider using other unknowns (e.g., y for x^2).

7. In geometry problems, consider using auxiliary lines.

8. For problems which are given in symbols, insert small numbers. This procedure helps to reduce the amount of abstract thinking necessary.

9. Can you solve a problem like the one you are given? Can you solve the problem if some aspect of it is changed? Consider extreme cases.

10. Try analyzing what is preventing you from reaching a solution. What do you need to know, or what must be done to solve the problem?

14.3 CARRY OUT THE PROCEDURE YOU HAVE DEVISED

For problems involving a numerical answer, it is a good idea to estimate an answer first. This estimate will help you to check your work later on.

Be sure to change all units to the same unit or system of units. Then do your calculations carefully, thinking at each step how they will help you arrive at what you are asked to find.

Neat, careful work provides three advantages: First, you are less likely to make a mistake. Second, if you should make a mistake, it will be easier to find. Third, the instructor can see what you do know and may give you partial credit even if the final answer is not correct.

It is possible to spend too much time doing calculations and not enough time demonstrating how much you know about calculus, physics, and so forth. Find out from your instructor how much he penalizes for arithmetical mistakes. If time is a factor, you may be better off actually *not* doing the calculation but indicating what you would do if you had the time; that is, outline your steps. Assign a symbol to the answer of what would be a long calculation and work with this symbol in the later stages of the solution to save time.

14.4 ACTIVELY CHECK YOUR ANSWER

Checking your answer must be more than just "going over" your work if it is to be highly effective in discovering mistakes. Effective checking procedures require the same quality of thought, the same searching questions and rigorous effort as was used originally to solve the problem.

Does your answer make sense? Is it reasonable? Does it agree with the estimate you made before you did the calculations?

If your answer is algebraic, can you substitute real numbers to see if you will get the correct answer? As one quantity increases (or decreases), does the algebraic expression behave as it should? Do you get correct values when extreme values are used? Is the answer in the correct units? For example, will an algebraic expression for volume of a geometric solid give you an answer in a cubic unit of measure?

Did you use all your data? If not, does it make sense to ignore certain data?

If your answer is not reasonable and you feel that you have made a mistake, try the problem again. Within any restrictions on time, work as independently of the first solution as possible. Do things differently. To guard against making the same mistake twice, refer only when necessary to your old solution or calculations. If you added a column of numbers from top to bottom the first time, add from bottom to top the second. If you multiplied and then divided the first time, divide first and multiply later. Watch carefully decimal points and units.

Analyze where the mistake may be. Is your answer off by a factor of 10? If so, look for a mistake in handling decimal points, exponents, and zeros. Is there an extra term which should be dropped out? Does the answer to an intermediate calculation make sense?

Finally, check to make sure the problem you have solved is actually the problem which was asked.

EXAMPLE OF HOW ONE STUDENT APPLIED THE PRINCIPLES IN THIS CHAPTER

Question: *A man goes into a store and buys* n *articles each having a list price of* c *cents. The store gives a discount of* p *percent on the list price. How many dollars does the man owe the storekeeper?*

I. Understand the problem.

What is required?

> *The number of dollars the man has to pay for the articles.*

What are the key terms?

> Each. *(Perhaps others too.)*

What will your answer look like?

> *An algebraic expression for the actual cost of the articles. The expression will be in terms of* n, p, *and* c.

II. Outline a procedure.

What do you know?

> *The number of articles,* n. *The cost of each article in cents,* c. *The percent of discount,* p.

What do you have to find?

> *The number of dollars the man has to pay for the articles.*

Use a good notation.

> *Let* A *be this actual total cost. (Note: The symbol* c *was not used again.)*

How will you get your answer?

I am stuck.

Did you use all your data?

Yes.

What can you find?

I can find how much he paid before the discount. But with a discount and change of units, it becomes more complex.

Let n = 3 articles, c = 50 cents, and p = 20%.

Use small numbers to reduce abstraction.

Cost is 3 × 50, or 150 cents or $1.50.

The discount is 20% of $1.50 or $.30.

The actual cost is $1.50 — $.30 or $1.20.

How will you get your answer?

I'll find the cost and change to dollars.

I'll then find the discount and subtract to get actual total cost.

III. Carry out the plan.

Find the cost before discounting.

$n \times c$

Change units to get cost in dollars.

$\dfrac{n \times c}{100}$

Find the discount.

$$p \times \left(\frac{n \times c}{100}\right) = \left(\frac{p}{100}\right) \times \left(\frac{n \times c}{100}\right)$$

Subtract the discount from the cost in dollars.

$$\frac{n \times c}{100} - \frac{p \times n \times c}{100 \times 100}$$

What is the answer?

$$A = \frac{n \times c}{100}\left(1 - \frac{p}{100}\right)$$

IV. Check the answer.

Does it work with real numbers?

$$Let\ n = 3$$
$$c = 50$$
$$p = 20$$

$$A = \frac{3 \times 50}{100}\left(1 - \frac{20}{100}\right)$$
$$= \frac{150}{100}\ (1 - .20)$$
$$= 1.50\ (.80)$$
$$= 1.20$$

Does the expression behave as it should?	*As n or c increases, A increases as it should.*
	As p increases, $\left(1 - \dfrac{p}{100}\right)$ *decreases and A decreases as it should.*
How about extreme values?	*When p = 0, A = undiscounted cost as it should; when p = 100, A = 0 as it should.*
Is the answer in correct units?	*Yes.* $\dfrac{n \times c}{100}$ *is in dollars.*
	$\left(1 - \dfrac{p}{100}\right)$ *has no units.*
	Thus dollars × no units = dollars—the correct unit for A.
Did you solve the problem that was asked?	*Yes, the problem wanted the actual cost in dollars—not the amount of the discount or some other value.*

———————————

15.

TESTS OF ABILITY TO READ GRAPHS

15.1 KNOW HOW TO READ BASIC GRAPHS

The graph at the right shows how many people there are on the average for each passenger car registered in five different countries.

To see how much you remember about graphs, try to find the answers to the following questions: (a) How many people are there for each passenger car registered in England? (b) Which one of the countries shown has the lowest

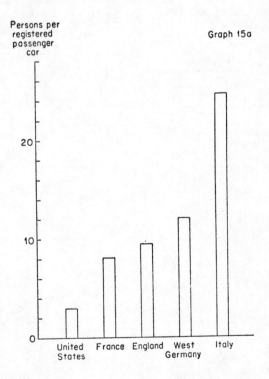

Persons per registered passenger car

Graph 15a

number of people for each registered passenger car? (c) Which country has 12.1 people for each registered passenger car? The answers are: (a) about 9.4, (b) United States, (c) West Germany.

If you had trouble answering these questions, we suggest that you review a chapter on graphs in an arithmetic book.

15.2 PAY CLOSE ATTENTION TO THE KEY FEATURES OF A GRAPH

a. *Title and labels on the axes.* Since a graph shows the relation among two or more variables, it is crucial to know precisely what these variables are. The title of the graph and the labels on the axes help to identify them.

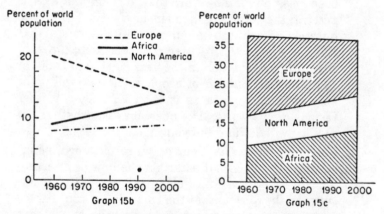

What are the variables in graph 15b? What might be a good title for this graph? Try to answer these questions before reading any further.

There are three variables involved in graph 15b; namely, percent of world population, year, and region of the world. A good title, therefore, would be: Percent of World Population from 1960–2000 for Three Regions of the World.

Answer yes or no to the following: Are fewer people expected to be living in Europe in the year 2000 than were living there in 1960? Use the data in graph 15b for your answer.

This is a much more difficult question than it appears. Certainly, the line representing Europe's data is going down from 1960 to 2000. But were you sufficiently observant to notice that the vertical axis is *percent* of world population? The graph shows that of all the people expected to be living in the world in the year 2000, a smaller *percentage* of them will be living in Europe when compared with the percent who lived in Europe in 1960.

The question asks about the *number* of people, not the *percentage*. If the axis had been *number* of people, then the answer to the question would have been yes. Since, however, the label on the axis is *percent*, the graph's data are insufficient to answer the question. From the graph we can determine that Europe is expected to have a smaller percentage of the world's population in the year 2000 than it did in 1960. But the *number* of people in Europe will probably continue to rise as it is in virtually all other regions of the world. The question asks whether the *number* will decline, and you should answer no.

b. *Scales on the axes.* Your graph readings will be inaccurate if you do not ascertain the unit of measurement used on the scales along the axes. If your answers to the questions at the beginning of the chapter were correct, then you must have been aware that each mark on the vertical axis of graph 15a represented an increase of two persons per registered passenger car over the mark immediately below it. What percent of the world population is represented by the difference between two adjacent marks in graph 15b? Since there are four evenly spaced marks for every 10 percentage points, it follows that each mark stands for 2½ percent more than the preceding one.

Notice, too, that on the horizontal axis the marks differ by ten-year intervals.

Make it a habit to locate the zero point on the vertical axis. When the zero value is not at the origin, some mistaken interpretations can occur.

For example, Graph 15a on page 124 indicates that Italy has slightly more than twice the number of persons per registered car than does West Germany (24.6 versus 12.1). The bar of Italy is slightly more than twice the height of that for West Germany.

If the vertical axis began at 8 instead of 0 (see the graph to the right), Italy would still have slightly more than twice the number of persons per registered car than does West Germany (24.6 versus 12.1). But the bar for Italy is *four times* the height of the one for West Germany.

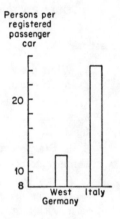

Persons per registered passenger car

Because the unsophisticated graph reader tends to compare the relative heights of bars (or lines) instead of the actual values, those who wish to deceive use graphs with a number other than zero as the origin or may use no units at all.

c. *Coding scheme.* In graph 15b separate codes are used to distinguish the change in percent of world population in Europe (- - -), Africa (—), and North America (—·—·—·). Be sure to keep this coding scheme straight to prevent a careless error.

d. *Base.* Two types of bases are frequently used in graphs appearing on examinations. Graph 15b has a "common" base because the percent values for each region are measured from the same (common) base, the horizontal axis, and thus can be read directly from the vertical scale.

Graph 15c, however, has an "additive" (or "composite") base in which the percent values for each region are *added* to those of the regions below it. To obtain a percent value for a given region (e.g., North America in 1960), the difference in the top and bottom percents (17 and 9) has to be obtained.

The common base graph is useful in that it highlights comparisons among the three regions. The additive graph illustrates more clearly the relative contribution of each region toward the *total* for the three regions combined.

Here are some questions based on graphs 15b and 15c. Since the graphs contain exactly the same data, you should check to see that you obtain the same answers from both graphs.

Questions

1. What percent of the world's population is expected to be living in Europe in the year 2000?
2. Which of the three regions is growing in population at about the same *rate* as the rest of the world? Prove it with figures.
3. Is the percent of the world's population living in these three regions expected to increase or decrease?
4. If the trend as shown continues beyond the year 2000, will Africa eventually have more people than Europe? (This is a tricky question. Answer true, false, or can't tell.)

Answers

1. 14 percent.
2. North America. This region had 8 percent of the world's population in 1960 and is expected to have 9 percent in 2000.
3. Decrease slightly. This can be seen most easily in graph 15c, where the total percent of the population in the three regions was 37 percent in 1960 and is expected to be 36 percent in 2000. The additive base graph is most helpful in answering questions like this. The total percent for most additive base graphs is 100 percent because all the components (regions of the world in our illustration) are usually shown.

4. True. If the predicted trend continues into the twenty-first century, a higher *proportion* of the world's population will live in Africa than will live in Europe. Therefore, more people will live in Africa than Europe. If you missed this question, you may have been thinking of a similar one in principle 15.2a, in which the point was made that you could not be sure of *absolute* numbers for a single region from one year to another. The present question, however, asked about *relative* figures for two regions at the same point in time.

15.3 ANSWER ACCORDING TO THE DATA SHOWN IN THE GRAPH, NOT BY A GUESS

Many standardized tests use the data in a graph as the basis for questions. Even though you feel you know the answer to a question without reference to the graph, check to make certain the data in the graph agree with your expectation.

The solution to many items based on graphs requires you to use other knowledge as well as data taken from the graph. Try this question which is based on graph 15a.

In England there is, on the average, one passenger car for about how many families? (a) 1 (b) 2 (c) 5 (d) 9.4

The answer to this question is not directly given in the graph. The graph does show that in England there are about 9.4 persons per registered passenger car. If you assume that most passenger cars are family owned and that the average family size is roughly 4 or 5, then option (b), one car for each two families, is the best answer.

This example was intended to illustrate how the data alone in a graph may not be sufficient to answer all questions. Another illustration is provided in the second practice problem below.

PROBLEMS FOR PRACTICE

The following examples represent a cross-section of the various types of more advanced graph-reading skills frequently tested. These questions and their answers should be studied carefully.

Set 1

Even though you may not have had a course in chemistry, you should be able to answer all the following questions based on the graph below. Such questions bring home the point that many test items based on graphs are primarily tests of your ability to read graphs and not tests of your knowledge of the subject matter contained in them.

The compressibility factor of methane as a function of pressure for three different temperatures

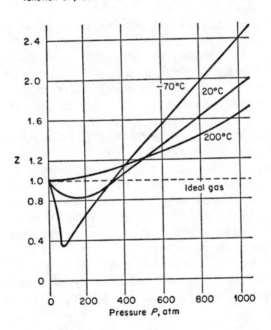

Questions (Set 1)

Your Answers:

a) What does Z stand for?

a) _____

b) At −70° C and 900 atmospheres of pressure, what is the compressibility factor of methane?

b) _____

c) For most pressures, as the temperature varies from 200° C to −70° C, is the compressibility factor of methane more or less like that for an ideal gas?

c) _____

d) At what pressure is the compressibility factor the same for methane at −70° C and methane at 20° C?

d) _____

e) For −70° C, at what pressure is the compressibility factor of methane one-half the compressibility at 600 atmospheres?

e) _____

f) What is the minimum compressibility factor of methane at 20° C, and at what pressure does this minimum occur?

f) _____

g) Between what pressures is the compressibility factor of methane at 20° C less than that of an ideal gas?

g) _____

h) For methane at −70° C at pressures between 100 and 1000 atmospheres, what is the rate of change of its compressibility factor?

h) _____

i) At pressures between 200 and 1000 atmospheres, the compressibility factor of methane is rising fastest at which temperature: −70° C, 20° C, or 200° C?

i) _____

Answers (Set 1)

a) From the title of the graph you should have been able to deduce that Z stands for the compressibility factor of methane.

b) This question requires you to read between the grid lines. The answer is approximately 2.2.

c) Less.

d) Zero and approximately 340 atmospheres, because that is where the two functions (lines) intersect.

e) At 600 atmospheres and −70° C, Z is about 1.55. A Z value of ½ of 1.55 (or .775) occurs at atmospheres of about 40 and 260 when the gas is at −70° C.

f) The curve for 20° C is lowest at a point just before 200 atmospheres. Z at this point is about 0.85.

g) The line for 20° C is below the line for an ideal gas between 0 and approximately 355 atmospheres.

h) Your estimate of this rate of change (slope) depends upon the range in which you choose to do your measurements, because the line is not *exactly* straight. For example, between 100 and 1000 atmospheres, Z increases about 2.0 for a rate of 2.0 per 900 atmospheres or .00222 per atmosphere. Between 800 and 1000 atmospheres, Z increases about .4 for a rate of .4 per 200 atmospheres or .00200 per atmosphere.

i) This question is asking for a comparison of three slopes. The steepest slope occurs at −70° C.

Set 2[1]

Many of the principles in this chapter apply to the reading of tables as well as to the reading of graphs. These questions are of a different type than those in Problem Set 1. Answer true or false.

Number of Persons Lynched in the United States

Year	Negro	White
1900–1904	471	61
1905–1909	337	40
1910–1914	294	29
1915–1919	230	33
1920–1924	193	29
1925–1929	50	21

Questions (Set 2)   *Your Answers*

a) There was an overall decline in the number of whites lynched during the first twenty-nine years of this century.   a) _____

[1] Parts of this example were adapted with permission from the *Illinois Test of Ability to Judge Interpretations of Data*, CIRCE, University of Illinois.

b) Probably more Negroes than whites were lynched during the latter half of the 1800s.

b) _____

c) The table shows that a greater number of Negroes than whites were lynched in 1927.

c) _____

d) The decline in the number of Negroes lynched since 1900 shows that white people have become more tolerant of Negroes.

d) _____

e) More than three times the *proportion* of Negroes to whites who live in the United States were lynched during the 1925–1929 period. (This is not an easy question.)

e) _____

Answers (Set 2)

a) True, in spite of the reversal from 29 to 33. The question asked about a tendency and not about a trend without exception.

b) True. One cannot be sure because data are not provided for the years in question. Extrapolation of the data certainly indicates a high probability that more Negroes were lynched than whites during those years.

c) False. Although it is probably true that more Negroes than whites were lynched in 1927, the table does not indicate this. The data are grouped by five-year periods; thus the results for any one year are not known.

d) False. White people *may* have become more tolerant of Negroes, but there are many other reasons why the number of Negro lynchings may have declined.

e) True. The question asks about proportion, not number. Since less than one-fourth of the persons living in the United States are Negro, the percent of Negroes lynched is greatly more than three times the percent of whites lynched. To answer this question correctly you needed to know something about the relative numbers of Negroes and whites living in the United States. See the last paragraph under principle 15.3.

PART 5

PRINCIPLES OF
TAKING SPECIAL
TYPES OF
EXAMINATIONS

This last part of the book deals with two important types of examinations, the open-book examination and the oral examination. In both of these, the kinds of test items used (Part III) and the nature of the abilities being measured (Part IV) may vary widely.

These two types should be closely studied: the open-book examination because of its expanding use, and the oral examination because many of the most important scholastic and professional decisions involving an individual are based either on this type of test, or the closely related interview.

16.

OPEN-BOOK
EXAMINATIONS

When taking an open-book examination, the student is permitted to use certain reference materials. Such materials may range from one sheet of paper containing notes to an unlimited number of books and pages of notes.

Open-book examinations, which measure your ability to organize and use data rather than to memorize them, are becoming popular in many areas of scholarship. These examinations closely approximate the normal problem-solving approach in real life where reference materials are readily available.

Since success in open-book examinations is tied directly to the *type of preparation* you make beforehand, it is necessary to shift our emphasis in this chapter from how to *take* tests to how to *prepare* for them.

16.1 DO YOUR LEARNING PRIOR TO THE EXAMINATION

Students taking an open-book examination for the first time usually fall into the trap of not studying as hard as they ordinarily would for regular tests. They reason that since they are taking an open-book test all they will need to do is refer to their textbooks and lecture notes and extract the answers.

The fallacy of this reasoning can be clearly seen through actual experiences of one of the authors. In his statistics courses open-book examinations make memorizing of formulas unnecessary and approximate more nearly real-life situations where statistics books are available. The questions on his examinations, like those on most open-book tests, do not have answers which can be found in a particular place in a textbook. Even questions which require the use of a formula presuppose an understanding of basic concepts before relevant formulas can be selected.

During these examinations, the poor students can be seen frantically reading the textbooks and shuffling through notes trying to learn material and find the answers. Much of their time is spent rejecting paragraph after paragraph and note after note as irrelevant. The good students, however, refer to their notes and book primarily as a check. Most of their time is spent writing and working directly on the examination. Again, the poor students run out of time, because most of their time is wasted trying to learn materials they should have learned prior to the examination.

16.2 ORGANIZE THE COURSE MATERIAL

One obvious way to save time is to organize (outline and index) the course material so that it can be retrieved quickly. In addition to saving time, the outlining and indexing suggested below have three other benefits. First, working with the main ideas and supporting material will aid in learning. Second, you will have outlines from which to extract material for your answers and will be less likely to leave out relevant ideas. Third, your textbook and notes will be more usable as future references after the course is over.

> a. *Index by topics in the course outline.* Make an outline of the topics covered in the course. You can use the outline furnished by the instructor as a start, or lacking this, you can list the main topics and subtopics contained in your class notes.

Next, write beside each topic and subtopic the page numbers indicating where the material can be found in both the textbook and your notebook. Figure 16.1 illustrates this system. You will notice in this figure that the instructor covered the topics in an order different from that found in the textbook and that material relevant to a given topic sometimes appears on several pages.

Notice also how the outline refers to two outside readings having relevance. Had notes on these supplementary references been placed in the notebook, the appropriate notebook page could have been indicated in the second column.

Computer-oriented Information Systems

	Textbook	*Notebook*
I. Major trends and directions	231–235; 276	68–69; 78–79
A. Indexing	231–233; 276	68; 78–79
B. Abstracting	233–235; 276	69; 78–79
II. Particular systems	236–273	70–78
A. KWIC	236–240	70–71
B. Selective dissemination	247–258	71–73
C. Citation indexes	241–247; 297	73–75; 78
D. Coordinate indexes } Note distinction between Case	258–264; 277–278	75–76; 78
E. Faceted classifications } Western Reserve Retrieval Thesaurus and U.S. Office of Education Thesaurus of Descriptors.	265–273; 277–278	76–78
III. The library of tomorrow	274–281	78–79

FIGURE 16.1 *Topic Outline*

---

b. *Index by themes.* When preparing for an open-book examination, it is worthwhile in some courses to construct additional outlines which coordinate material from many different sections of the textbook and notes. In a mathematics or science course such an outline could contain a listing of the main formulas, processes, or procedures together with corresponding pages. In other courses outlines could be organized around key questions. An example of an outline based on key questions is shown in Figure 16.2. Notice in this figure how the outside reading or reference material has been incorporated in the outline.

16.3 AVOID LENGTHY TEXTBOOK QUOTATIONS IN YOUR ANSWERS

Avoid transferring a paragraph verbatim from the textbook to your examination paper for the following reasons: First, a paragraph as it stands in the textbook may pertain to the question, but it may not be the precise emphasis required by the question; second, a copied paragraph is devoid of any personal contribution; third, any student, poor or good, can copy from the textbook; and fourth, you may be wasting valuable time.

We suggest that a pertinent paragraph be condensed. Phrase the main ideas in your own words, tie the ideas to the question by using appropriate phrases from the question itself, and provide the instructor with page and paragraph numbers in parentheses.

16.4 DO NOT OVER-ANSWER THE QUESTION

Avoid the temptation of going overboard in your answer—a temptation caused by having your notes, textbook, and other pertinent materials available. Select and present concisely only that information which is needed for a full answer. In brief, understand the question and then write to the point. The importance of writing to the point and handling material

Question: How will information be controlled in the future?

	Textbook	*Notebook*
I. Key problem in controlling information is getting it properly indexed.	69–73	3–4
A. Information can be retrieved rapidly only if it is properly indexed.	73–76	5–7
B. Large volume of information—reports, memos, pamphlets, etc.	125–130	8–10
C. No one person can absorb all the information in one field to catalog it in one language.	80–81	12–13
1. Reference retrieval.	89–91	11–12
2. Fact retrieval.	92–93	13–14
3. Specific problem.	95–99	15–16
D. Different retrieval systems needed for consumer versus researcher (see reference by Barhydt).	101–105	17
II. What information is worth storing?	125–126	19
A. In a fast developing country or field of knowledge the most valuable information is in the recent bulletins, documents, etc., and not in books.	130–135	20–21
B. Very costly to read all technical literature and file by topic, author, or main points of interest.	137–138	23
C. Much fugitive material is not worth storing.	140–141	22
III. Solution: Not developed.		
A. Compatibility of retrieval systems to each other (see Beck reference).	141–142	24–25
B. Get trained people to catalog information.	142	25
C. Machines can handle it, but man cannot get it into the machines.	143–144	26
D. Mechanism needed to make selection of what gets stored.	144–146	26–28

FIGURE 16.2   *Theme Outline*

of dubious relevance is discussed in principle 6.4 beginning on page 45.

The dangers in over-answering a question include detracting from the important points and wasting valuable time. Wasting time is a concern expressed repeatedly in this chapter.

17.

**ORAL
EXAMINATIONS**
(And Interviews)

During an oral examination the questions are usually asked by one or more instructors. Though the opening questions are generally formulated in advance, the subsequent ones are usually spontaneous, arising out of immediate responses. The objective of these probing questions is to ascertain the strengths and weaknesses of the individual, as well as the depth and breadth of his ideas. Through this type of continuous give-and-take an examination may be shaped to the individual. Oral examinations are very time-consuming, but their value is precisely that they can be shaped to the individual.

Since most major examinations in both college and the business world are oral, the principles which pertain to oral examinations deserve serious study. In a very real sense, an interview may be considered as a kind of oral examination. During a job interview, for example, your answers to a series of questions determine whether you pass, that is, get the position.

The principles in this chapter are applicable to both situations—oral examinations and interviews.

17.1 INQUIRE BEFOREHAND ABOUT THE SCOPE OF THE EXAMINATION

Though large blocks of time are often allotted for oral examinations, there is seldom enough time for the instructor to ask everything that he would like. Consequently, the instructor will be selective in deciding the subject areas he will emphasize. Most will reveal these areas if you only ask; often you will be surprised to learn that the intended coverage does not include areas which you had planned for intensive study. Getting this information beforehand will help you to make the best possible use of your preexamination time.

17.2 BE A GOOD LISTENER

There are two reasons why it is important to be a good listener. First, you are less likely to misinterpret questions. An answer to a question or point not raised or a missing slant or emphasis will immediately give the instructor the impression that you think imprecisely.

Second, if you are a good listener you will not monopolize the conversation. Remember that the examination should not be a monologue; more often than not, mature restraint leaves a positive impression.

During periods of listening, we suggest that you use a pad of paper to record ideas that come to mind which you do not want to forget, and to record suggestions and recommendations made by the instructor.

17.3 ASK QUESTIONS TO CLARIFY THE ORIGINAL QUESTION

One of the most important things you can do during oral examinations is to ask the instructor questions to make certain you understand not only his questions, but also the kind of answers he desires. It is not unusual for the questions which the instructor asks on the spur of the moment to be vague and ambiguous. Requesting clarification will not only help you in formulating a good answer; it will also convey a reflective rather than impulsive approach to problems.

17.4 THINK BEFORE YOU SPEAK

When you have much to say in answer to a question, pause a few moments to organize it. (Making notes on paper will help you remember and organize the points you want to make.) Instructors will always give you a reasonable amount of time to think before you answer. When you do start to answer, choose your words carefully. In an oral examination, unlike a written one, false starts cannot be erased.

17.5 DO NOT CONFESS COMPLETE IGNORANCE

It is extremely rare that you will know nothing about a topic. If you can only say a little in answer to a question, say the little that you know. Your instructor may follow up a short answer with additional questions which may be suggestive and consequently easier to answer.

17.6 DO NOT BLUFF

Your instructors will probably recognize bluffing for what it is, and you will be worse off for bluffing than if you merely had said something like: "I'm sorry that I cannot give a full answer, but here is the very little which may be pertinent." When such a statement has been made, every correct fact which you present looms positive and large.

17.7 DO NOT PAD EXCESSIVELY

No one likes to listen to a monologue of irrelevant utterances. If you have a sincere doubt whether or not a lengthy description or explanation is desired, then say something like: "I am prepared to discuss *this* and *that* phase of the topic if you want me to."

17.8 IDENTIFY OPINIONS AND GUESSES, AND DEFEND THEM

On some oral examinations considerable time is spent on questions which do *not* have a correct answer. For these questions, the instructor is interested not only in your opinion, but also in your defense of that opinion.

In your answers, make clear what you regard as personal opinions. Support these with reasons. If there are other plausible opinions, mention them and indicate their strong and weak points.

If you can't think of a good answer to a question then take a guess—but tell the instructor you are guessing. If you are wrong, you are no worse off than if you had said nothing. If you are correct, your answer is sure to be that much more impressive and might be interpreted as a good example of "thinking on your feet."

17.9 HAVE GOOD MANNERS

In many oral examinations and job interviews it is often true that what you say is less important than how you say it and how you behave. Your instructors' future recommendations of you will be based in large measure on their overall impressions of you as a person and as a student. Soon after an oral examination or interview the examiner may forget the questions he asked and the answers you gave; but he will long remember your appearance, your attitude, and your approach in dealing with questions.

Try to maintain a good balance between a natural informality and a polite, respectful reserve. Do not give the appearance of nonchalance by sitting in a slouched position or by giving flippant or arrogant answers. Oral examinations are not routine. They should be treated as serious, even momentous.

It is essential to be well dressed and well groomed. A slovenly appearance may be interpreted as a lack of respect for the examiner and a low regard for the occasion itself.

Do not interrupt, and be quick to beg someone's pardon for any slip.

The best preparation you can make for an oral examination is to know your subject. But once in the examination or interview setting, the best action you can take is to be certain your behavior is reflective, polite, and dignified.

"Have good manners" illustrates many of the principles in this book. Although this statement is most relevant for the type of examination discussed in this chapter, it is also a good rule to follow in other test-taking situations. For example, bad manners such as making noise and getting up often to sharpen pencils often disturb others and do not permit you to "use your time wisely."

A FINAL WORD

In writing this book, we adopted the premise that every individual is important and deserves to have his understandings, skills, and capabilities accurately and fairly judged. In our society, the best way to make these judgments is to look at what an individual can accomplish on carefully selected tasks and compare this with the accomplishments of others or with given standards. These accomplishments, an individual's performance, are often observed under test conditions.

Unfortunately, tests are fallible measuring devices; measurement is made inaccurate by many factors which suppress an individual's true ability. The absence of knowledge of how to take tests is one such factor. The goal of our work is to help the real-you perform and be assessed.

APPENDIXES

APPENDIX 1

KEY TERMS

1. INTRODUCTION

This appendix deals with two categories of *key terms:* first, key terms of *procedure and direction;* and second, key terms of *quantity and degree.* The key terms of procedure and direction are divided into five subcategories: *identification, description, relation, demonstration,* and *evaluation.* The key terms of quantity and degree are made up of two subcategories: *exact* and *indefinite.*

When used in test directions and questions, these terms must be not only *noticed,* but also *interpreted* accurately in order for you to give a precise answer. To ensure that you notice these key terms, we recommend that you place circles around them. As for interpretation, always use the standard meanings in the context of the subject matter except when an instructor, because of personal idiosyncrasy, uses them in an unusual and private sense. (Previous references to key terms may be found under principles 4.7, 6.1a, 6.1c, 8.9, and 8.10.)

2. KEY TERMS OF PROCEDURE AND DIRECTION

a. *Identification.* These words direct you to present the bare facts: a name, a phrase, a date; in short, to provide a concise answer.

IDENTIFICATION TERMS

cite	*indicate*
define	*list*
enumerate	*mention*
give	*name*
identify	*state*

Notice in the following example that nine of the key terms have just about the same meaning.

Indicate (*cite, enumerate, give, identify, list, mention, name, state*) four conditions which exist in a period of depression.

An acceptable answer to the above question is:

(1) Widespread unemployment, (2) low gross national product, (3) low interest rates, and (4) very low and sometimes negative capital investment.

Avoid the error of launching into a long essay, *describing* rather than *listing*. Remember that these *identification* words are your clue that a concise answer is wanted.

b. *Description.* These words direct you to tell about a specific topic with a certain amount of detail.

DESCRIPTION TERMS

describe	*illustrate*
discuss	*sketch*
review	*develop*
summarize	*outline*
diagram	*trace*

The following is an example of a question using the descriptive term, *discuss.*

Discuss the following statement. Since the reformation, three powers have attempted to dominate Europe: France, Spain, and Germany. Of these, France proved to be the most successful.

An answer to this question should be fairly detailed. If the term *comment on* instead of *discuss* had been used, a somewhat shorter answer might have been expected. A sample outline of an answer to this question follows,

I. Attempts at domination

A. SPAIN	B. FRANCE	C. GERMANY
1. Charles V	1. Louis XIV	1. Frederick the Great
2. Philip II	2. Napoleon	2. Bismarck
	3. Louis Napoleon	3. Kaiser Wilhelm
		4. Hitler

II. Reasons for French success
   A. Geographical
   B. Unified state
   C. Degree of social progress
   D. Cultural supremacy

The emphasis which is given to a description depends upon the slant demanded by the key term. For example, the terms *describe* and *discuss* permit wide freedom in organizing an answer. These terms may be interpreted safely to mean "write a good essay about."

Review and *summarize* mean "bring out the main points." *Diagram, illustrate,* and *sketch* may mean "make a drawing." Depending on the context of the question as intended by the examiner, *illustrate* may also mean "give one or more examples," and *sketch* may also mean "outline."

Three terms which direct you to organize your answer by an appropriate *sequence* of events or ideas are *develop, outline,* and *trace.* The important consideration here is not to lose the path of the sequence in a thicket of details, or to follow up side issues which detract from the progress of your answer.

c. *Relation.* These words direct you to describe the similarities, differences, or associations between two or more subjects.

RELATION TERMS

analyze	*differentiate*
compare	*distinguish*
contrast	*relate*

There are subtle differences among the relation terms listed above which are not always adhered to by the test maker. When the word *compare* is used, the test taker is usually wise to bring out *both* similarities and differences between the subjects. However, with the words *contrast*, *differentiate*, and *distinguish* the emphasis is clearly upon the *differences*.

There is no single length of answer or degree of detail which is required when relation terms are used. You must be guided by the rest of the examination, the specific subject, and the intent of the examiner. An example of a question using a relation term is:

Differentiate between political faction and political party.

To answer this question a student wrote the following short, but *differentiating* description.

A faction is a political group organized for a specific purpose and is usually against the interests of the majority.

A political party is also a political group, but it is a more permanent institution of people with many more interests than a faction and has as its main goal winning elections.

---

d. *Demonstration.* These terms direct you to show (not state) why something is true or false. You must put forth evidence or arguments to support a specific statement, and your argument must be logical.

DEMONSTRATION TERMS

demonstrate	*prove*
explain why	*show*
justify	*support*

These key terms of demonstration are most frequently used in mathematics tests, as in the following item.

Prove, (show, demonstrate) that the sum of the square of any number and the square of its reciprocal is always greater than or equal to 2.

One approach to answering this question would be to use calculus. The values of n (any number), when the first derivative of the function $[f'(n)]$ is set equal to zero, are those numbers for which the value of the function is an extreme. A positive sign of the second derivative $[f''(n)]$ evaluated at the point n indicates the extreme is a minimum. A specific answer might be,

Let n = any number. It is required to prove that $f(n) \geqq 2$ where $f(n) = n^2 + n^{-2}$.

    A. To find an extreme value for the function,

$$f'(n) = 2n - 2n^{-3} = 0$$
$$n = 1, -1$$
$$f(1) = (1)^2 + (1)^{-2} = 2$$
$$f(-1) = (-1)^2 + (-1)^{-2} = 2$$

Thus, 2 is the extreme value.

    B. To check if this extreme value is a minimum,

$$f''(n) = 2 + 6n^{-4}$$
$$f''(1) = 2 + 6 = 8$$
$$f''(-1) = 2 + 6 = 8$$

Since the second derivative shows a positive value, 2 is the minimum value that the function can have.

e. *Evaluation.* The evaluation terms ask for your opinion or judgment on a subject. Your opinion, however, is only part of the requirement; how you justify and support it is the other part. Be sure to appraise both sides of a subject, especially if there is an obvious objection which can be raised about your point of view. (*Criticize* means "point out good as well as bad points.")

EVALUATION TERMS

assess	*evaluate*
comment	*interpret*
criticize	*propose*

3. KEY TERMS OF QUANTITY AND DEGREE

a. *Exact.* Wherever exact terms are used, they mean 0 percent or 100 percent of the time. A single exception makes an *all* or a *never* statement false (review principles 8.9 and 8.10).

EXACT TERMS
all	*necessarily*
always	*never*
must	*no/none*
	without exception

b. *Indefinite.* This partial list of terms of an indefinite quantity or degree is arranged in rough order from little to much. *Regularly*, which is not included, implies a predictable and periodic occurrence which may be frequent or infrequent.

INDEFINITE TERMS

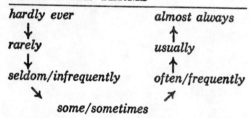

There is a great deal of judgment involved in whether or not a particular event occurs frequently enough to be classified by any one of the terms shown above. It is best to answer as you think the test maker intended.

APPENDIX 2

PREFIXES

COMMON PREFIXES (ASSIMILATED)

A final consonant of a prefix is frequently changed to combine with the initial consonant of the root which immediately follows. Occasionally the final consonant is dropped. This changing and dropping is called *assimilation*, and it structures the English word making it easier to pronounce. For example, *in* becomes *il-* in *illegible*.

The prefixes in the following list are most frequently subjected to assimilation and have, at least, several variant forms.

Prefix	Meaning	Example	Definition
ab-	away from	abnormal	away from the average
a-	away from	amorphous	without shape
abs-	away from	absolve	to free from
ad-	to, toward	adhere	to stick to
a-	to, toward	abut	to push
ac-	to, toward	accumulate	to heap up
af-	to, toward	affiliate	to unite closely
ag-	to, toward	aggravate	to intensify
al-	to, toward	allure	to entice
an-	to, toward	announce	to report
ap-	to, toward	appose	to place opposite
ar-	to, toward	arrogate	to make undue claims
as-	to, toward	assault	to attack
at-	to, toward	attenuate	to make thin, weaken
contra-	against	contradict	to assert the contrary of
contro-	against	controvert	to oppose with arguments
counter-	against	countermand	to revoke a command
co-	together, with	coexist	to exist together
col-	together, with	collaborate	to work together
com-	together, with	compose	to form by putting together
con-	together, with	conglomerate	to collect into a mass
cor-	together, with	corrugate	to form into folds
dis-	separation,	disassemble	to take apart
di-	reversal,	diametric	directly adverse
dif-	negation	diffuse	to spread widely
ex-	out of, out from	expel	to drive out
e-	out of, out from	evacuate	to empty of contents
ec-	out of, out from	eccentric	out of center
ef-	out of, out from	effusive	pouring out, gushing
in-	in, within	incorporate	to unite

Prefix	Meaning	Example	Definition
em-	in, within	empathy	projections of one's own feelings
en-	in, within	engage	to involve
il-	in, within	illuminate	to make light
im-	in, within	immerse	to plunge into
ir-	in, within	irrigate	to supply with water
in-	not	inanimate	not endowed with life
ig-	not	ignoble	not noble
il-	not	illegible	not legible
im-	not	immature	not mature
ir-	not	irrational	not according to reason
ob-	against	obstruct	to work or build against
of-	against	offend	to strike against
op-	against	opponent	one that opposes
sub-	under, from under	submerge	to put under water
suf-	under, from under	suffumigate	to fumigate from below
syn-	together, with	synthesis	a putting together
syl-	together, with	syllable	a unit of several letters together
sym-	together, with	sympathy	an association bound with feeling

COMMON PREFIXES (ADDITIONAL)

Prefix	Meaning	Example	Definition
bene-	good, well	benevolence	disposition to do good
bi-	two, twice	biannual	occurring twice a year
circum-	around	circumlocution	talking around a point
extra-	beyond	extrasensory	beyond ordinary sense perception
intra-	within	intravenous	within a vein
intro-	within	introspect	to look within one's own mind
mal-	bad, evil	malevolent	disposition to do evil
multi-	many	multiped	having many feet
over-	above	overprice	to charge over the normal price
post-	after	posthumous	occurring after one's death
retro-	backward	retrospect	looking back on things past
semi-	half	semicircle	a half circle
super-	above, over	supernatural	above or beyond nature
tri-	three	triad	a group of three
ultra-	beyond	ultramodern	beyond the norm of the modern

PREFIXES FOUND IN SCIENTIFIC AND TECHNICAL WORDS

Prefix	Meaning	Example	Definition
a-	not, without	aphonic	having no sound
an-	not, without	anelectric	not becoming electrified by friction
ana-	upward, again	anadromous	ascending rivers, from the sea for breeding, as shad
apo-	from, away	apochromatic	free from chromatic and spherical aberration
cata-	down, away	cataplasia	regressive change in cells
dys-	ill, hard	dysphagia	difficulty in swallowing
ecto-	outside	ectoparasite	parasite living on exterior of animals
endo-	within	endoskeleton	an internal skeleton
eu-	good, well	euphoria	a sense of well-being
exo-	outside	exoskeleton	an external skeleton
hemi-	half	hemicycle	a half circle
hetero-	different	heterochromatic	having a complex pattern of colors
iso-	equal, alike	isomagnetic	indicating equality of magnetic force
macro-	large	macrocosm	the great world
mega-	great, million	megalith	a huge stone used in prehistoric monuments
meso-	middle	mesothorax	the middle of the three segments of the thorax of an insect
met-	after, between, change	metathorax	the middle segment of the thorax in insects
meta-	after, between, change	metamorphosis	change of form
micro-	small	microcosm	a small world
neo-	new	neolithic	new stone age
pan-	all	panchromatic	sensitive to all colors
para-	beside	parathyroid	glands beside the thyroid
peri-	around	perimeter	the outer boundary
poly-	many	polychrome	many-colored
proto-	first	prototype	the original or first model
pseudo-	false	pseudopod	false foot
tele-	far	telepathy	communication from one mind to another

APPENDIX 3
ROOTS AND COMBINING FORMS

ROOTS AND COMBINING FORMS TAKEN FROM LATIN NOUN AND ADJECTIVE ROOTS

Root or Combining Form	Meaning	Example	Definition
aero-	air	aerodromics	the science of flying aircraft
agr-	field	agronomy	the study of soils and field-crop production
alb-	white	albino	an organism lacking normal pigment in the skin
ampli-	large	ampliation	an enlargement
ann(u)-	year	annuity	money payable yearly
api-	bee	apiary	place where bees are kept
avi-	bird	aviary	a place for keeping birds confined
bell-	war	bellicose	warlike
bene-	good, well	beneficence	active goodness, kindness, charity
carn-	flesh	carnivorous	preying or feeding on animals
clar-	clear	clarity	clearness
copi-	abundance	copious	plentiful
cord-	heart	cordial	sincere; from the heart
corpus-	body	corpulent	bulky; very fat
cupr-	copper	cupreous	containing copper
dent-	tooth	dentiform	tooth-shaped
digit-	finger	digitate	resembling fingers
equi-	even	equidistant	equally distant
fabul-	story	fabulous	like a fable, especially in exaggeration
flor-	flower	floriferous	bearing flowers
foli-	leaf	foliate	leafy
fort-	strong	fortitude	firmness of mind in adversity
frat-	brother	fraternize	to hold fellowship as brothers
greg-	flock	gregarious	tending to flock or herd together
herb-	grass	herbivorous	eating or living on plants
ig-	fire	igneous	containing fire
irid-	rainbow	iridescence	a rainbow play of colors
lact-	milk	lactescent	having a milky look
lingu-	tongue, language	linguist	a person skilled in languages
loc-	place	locality	a place
magni-	great, big	magnify	make bigger
mal-	bad	malnutrition	bad nutrition
man(u)-	hand	manuscript	written by hand
mor-	custom	mores	customs having ethical significance

Root or Combining Form	Meaning	Example	Definition
mort-	death	mortuary	a place where dead bodies are kept before burial
multi-	many	multilateral	many-sided
omni-	all	omnipresent	present everywhere at once
pac-	peace	pacify	to make peaceful
pecuni-	money	pecuniary	consisting of money
petr-	rock	petrify	to change into stone
pisci-	fish	piscatorial	pertaining to fishes
plen-	full	replenish	to fill again
plumb-	lead (metal)	plumbiferous	producing or containing lead
pomi-	apple, fruit	pomology	science of fruit growing
popul-	people	populous	densely populated
prim-	first	primogeniture	(Law) an exclusive right of inheritance belonging to the first-born
radi-	ray	radiant	vividly shining
sanct-	holy	sanctimonious	making a show of sanctity
semin-	seed	seminal	germinal, originative
sen-	old	senile	characteristic of old age
silv-	forest	sylvan	pertaining to forests
soli-	alone	soliloquy	the act of talking to oneself
somni-	sleep	somnambulate	to walk when asleep
tempor-	time	temporize	to comply with the time or occasion
terra-	earth	territory	large tract of land
umbra-	shade	umbrella	a guard for sheltering one from sun, rain
verm-	worm	vermicular	wormlike in form or motion

ROOTS AND COMBINING FORMS TAKEN FROM LATIN VERB ROOTS

Root or Combining Form	Meaning	Example	Definition
acr-	sour	acrimony	sharpness or bitterness
ambul-	walk	ambulatory	walking; moving about
aug-	increase	augment	increase in size, amount, or degree
cant-	sing	cantabile	in a singing manner
cant-	sing	cantata	a choral composition
-ced	move	preceding	going before in time or order
-ced	move	proceed	to move forward
-cess	move	procession	a group moving on in orderly manner
cern-	separate	discern	to identify as separate and distinct
clam-	cry out	exclaim	to speak in sudden emotion
clud-	close	preclude	to shut out by anticipation
clus-	close	recluse	shut up from the world
cresc-	grow	crescendo	a gradual increase in volume of sound
dic-	say	predict	to tell beforehand
dorm-	sleep	dormant	sleeping; inactive; latent
-flect	bend	genuflect	to bend the knee
flex-	bend	flexible	pliable; not rigid
grad-	step	gradual	proceeding by steps or degrees
gred-	step	ingredient	that which enters into a compound
horr-	shudder at	horrendous	frightful
hum-	be moist	humidify	to moisten
langu-	feel weak	languor	lack of vigor
laud-	praise	laudable	praiseworthy
loqui-	talk	loquacious	given to talking
locut-	talk	elocution	style of speaking in public
migr-	depart	migratory	roving
monstr-	show	demonstrate	to show outwardly
mov-	move	immovable	steadfast; unyielding
mot-	move	motile	capable of movement
mut-	change	mutable	capable of sudden variation
mutat-	change	mutation	a sudden variation
nomin-	name	nominal	existing in name only
nominat-	name	nominate	to name a candidate
pend-	hang	pendulous	hanging or swinging
-prehend	seize	apprehend	to arrest; to perceive
prehens-	seize	prehensile	adapted for seizing or grasping

Root or Combining Form	Meaning	Example	Definition
rupt-	break	rupture	a breaking apart
-rupt	break	interrupt	to break into
-sci-	know	conscious	aware or sensible
-scope	see	telescope	an optical instrument to aid the eye in seeing distant objects
sed-	sit	sedentary	accustomed to sit much
-sess	sit	session	sitting of a group
sent-	feel	sentiment	feeling; emotion
sens-	feel	sensitive	having quick and acute feelings
sequ-	follow	sequential	following in order
-secut	follow	consecutive	following one another
-serv	keep, save	preserve	to keep intact
-sid	sit down	reside	to dwell permanently
-sist	stand	insist	to take a stand
sud-	sweat	sudorific	causing or inducing sweat
tang-	touch	tangible	capable of being touched
tact-	touch	tactile	perceptible by the touch
-teg-	cover	integument	external coating or skin
-tect	cover	protect	to shield from injury
tend-	stretch	extend	to stretch or draw out
tens-	stretch	tension	act of stretching
torp-	numb	torpid	having lost feeling; dormant
turg-	swell	turgid	inflated; swollen; bloated
-ven	come	convene	to come together in a body
viv-	live	viviparous	producing living young (instead of eggs) from within the body
voc-	call	vociferous	making a loud out ry
vocat-	call	vocation	a calling to a particular profession
-volv	roll	revolve	to turn over and over

ROOTS AND COMBINING FORMS FOUND IN SCIENTIFIC AND TECHNICAL WORDS

Root or Combining Form	Meaning	Example	Definition
actin-	ray	actinology	the science of rays of light
arthr-	joint	arthritis	inflammation of the joints
astr-	star	astronomy	the science of celestial bodies
auto-	self	automaton	a person acting mechanically
cac-	diseased	cachexia	a condition of ill health
cardi-	heart	cardiology	the science of the heart
cephal-	head	cephalous	having a head
chrom-	color	chromatology	the science of colors
cosm-	world	cosmometry	science of measuring universe
cry-	frost	cryogeny	science of refrigeration
cyt-	cell	cytology	science of dealing with cells
derm-	skin	dermatology	the science of the skin
dyn-	power	dynamometry	process of measuring forces
ethno-	race	ethnology	the science dealing with the division of mankind into races
geo-	earth	geostatic	pressure exerted by the earth
ger-	old age	geriatrics	medicine concerned with old age and its diseases
heli-	sun	heliotrope	a plant which turns toward the sun
hem(at)-	blood	hemophilia	a tendency, usually hereditary, to profuse bleeding even from slight wounds
hepat-	liver	hepatitis	inflammation of the liver
hier-	sacred	hieroglyphic	sacred character in picture writing of ancient Egyptians
hydr-	water	hydrography	the study of bodies of water
hygr-	moisture	hygrometer	apparatus for measuring moisture
nephr-	kidney	nephritis	inflammation of the kidneys
neur-	nerve	neuritis	inflammation of a nerve
odont-	tooth	odontology	science of the teeth
ortho-	straight	orthodox	conventional in opinion or doctrine
phot-	light	phototonus	sensitiveness to light
pneum(on)-	lung	pneumonia	a disease of the lungs
pneumat-	air, wind	pneumatic	moved by pressure of air
pyr-	fire	pyrometer	instrument for measuring high temperatures

Root or Combining Form	Meaning	Example	Definition
rhin-	nose	rhinology	medicine dealing with treatment of the nose
therm-	heat	thermo-anesthesia	inability to distinguish heat or cold by touch
xyl-	wood	xylophone	a percussion instrument of wooden bars

APPENDIX 4

SUFFIXES

SUFFIXES COMMONLY USED TO FORM ADJECTIVES

Suffix	Usual Meaning	Example	Meaning
-able	capable of	flammable	capable of being easily ignited
-al	belonging to	autumnal	belonging to autumn
-ant	characterized by	recalcitrant	characterized by being stubbornly rebellious
-en	made of	oaken	made of oak
-ent	characterized by	diffident	characterized by extreme timidity
-esque	in the style of	Romanesque	in the style resembling the Roman
-ful	full of	careful	full of care
-ible	capable of	flexible	capable of being bent
-ic	pertaining to	romantic	pertaining to romance
-ile	showing	senile	showing habits of old age
-ine	like, belonging to	feminine	like a woman
-ious	full of	invidious	full of ill-feeling
-ish	like, typical of	peevish	showing ill temper
-ive	the nature of	offensive	giving offense
-less	without	careless	without care
-ly	like	scholarly	like a learned person
-oid	like	anthropoid	resembling man; applied especially to certain apes
-ory	pertaining to	sensory	pertaining to the senses
-ous	having qualities of	famous	qualities of fame
-some	full of	troublesome	full of trouble
-ward	toward	windward	toward the wind
-y	like	milky	like milk

SUFFIXES COMMONLY USED TO FORM VERBS

Suffix	Usual Meaning	Example	Meaning
-en	to make	lighten	to make lighter
-fy	to make	amplify	to make more ample
-ize	to make	popularize	to make popular

SUFFIXES COMMONLY USED TO FORM FEMININE WORDS

Suffix	Example	Meaning
-ess	lioness	a female lion
-ette	suffragette	a woman advocate of suffrage for her sex
-ine	heroine	a woman of heroic spirit
-ess	poetess	a woman poet
-trix	aviatrix	a woman pilot of an airplane

SUFFIXES COMMONLY USED TO SHOW THE AGENT

Suffix	Usual Meaning	Example	Meaning
-ant	one who	servant	one who serves
-ard	one who	drunkard	one who often gets drunk
-ary	one devoted to	missionary	one devoted to missions
-er	one who	racer	one who races
-eer	one who deals in	profiteer	one who deals in profits
-ent	one who	president	one who presides
-ist	one who practices	dentist	one who practices dentistry
-or	one engaged in	actor	one engaged in acting

SUFFIES COMMONLY USED TO ...

Suffix	Usua...		DA...
-age	quality of		
-ance	act or qual...		
-cy	act or ...		
-dom	quali... state o...		
-ence	quality o...		
-ery	state of		
-hood	state of	c...	
-ice	state of	justi...	
-ion	act of	commun...	
-ism	act of	favoritism	
-ity	state of	purity	s... co...
-ment	state of	amazement	state o...
-ness	quality of	goodness	quality of ...
-ship	process of	statesmanship	paying attenti... of state
-sion	process of	comprehension	process of compreh... understanding
-th	state of	width	state of being wide
-tion	state of	attention	state of heeding
-tude	state of	amplitude	state of being ample
-ure	act of	exposure	act of exposing

SUFFIXES COMMONLY USED TO FORM DIMINUTIVES

Suffix	Example	Meaning
-cle	fascicle	a small bundle
-et	lancet	a small lance
-ette	cigarette	a little roll of tobacco
-ie	lassie	a small girl or lass
-kin	lambkin	a young lamb
-let	droplet	a minute drop
-ling	duckling	a young duck
-ock	bullock	a young bull
-ule	cellule	a small cell